THE COMPANY TOWN IN THE AMERICAN WEST

THE COMPANY TOW

N THE AMERICAN WEST

by James B. Allen

UNIVERSITY OF OKLAHOMA PRESS
NORMAN

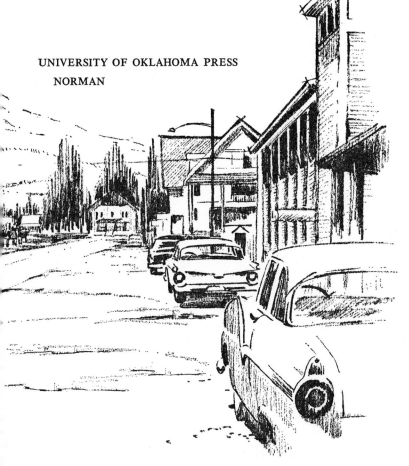

LIBRARY OF CONGRESS CATALOG CARD NUMBER: 66–13420

Copyright 1966 by the University of Oklahoma Press, Publishing Division of the University. Composed and printed at Norman, Oklahoma, U.S.A., by the University of Oklahoma Press. First edition.

DEDICATED TO *Donald C. Cutter*
TEACHER AND FRIEND

A N IMPORTANT ASPECT of American economic and social history which has received little formal attention from historians is the rise and decline of the company-owned town. The literature of American history is punctuated with accounts of many kinds of communities: the New England village, the socialistic Utopian community, the frontier outfitting post, the rough-and-tumble mining camp, the cow town of the Great Plains, the Mormon village in the Great Basin, and, in modern times, the big city and its sprawling suburbs. Each of these different types of communities has had its story told, and each story has become a familiar part of the general picture of American development. Almost neglected, however, has been the company-owned town. Hundreds of these relatively isolated, one-industry communities have dotted all parts of the American map, and some are still playing important roles in the economic life of their particular regions.

How and why did company towns develop in America? How extensive has been the existence of such towns, and how many are still functioning? Was the development of particular industries in any way dependent upon company-owned communities? What special problems came to the companies by virtue of their positions as landlords and town governments? What special advantages did management have, or take, because of company-town ownership? How was the life of an employee in a company town different from life in another kind of community? What effect have changing economic conditions had upon the company town as an institution? Why are these towns disappearing?

With such questions in mind a study of the company town in one of the large geographic regions of the United States seems worth while. To study all such towns in the country would be an overwhelming task, and to study only a few would limit the treatment to such an extent that it would be relatively insignificant in the context of American history. Taking a particular region, however, gives opportunity to develop a picture with some national significance and also leaves space to deal with some of the more interesting aspects of particular communities. Since the Far West seems to form a natural geographic section for this study, the states of Washington, Oregon, California, Nevada, Idaho, Montana, Utah, Wyoming, Colorado, Arizona, and New Mexico have been considered. Nearly two hundred company-owned towns have been identified in these eleven states alone.

A Note on Sources

The problem of locating company-owned towns was surprisingly complicated, and it is a certainty that not all of them have been found. Residents and managers of existing towns were contacted and asked for suggestions, as well as trade associations, state mining departments, state historical societies, unions, the federal government, forestry and mining departments of various universities, and a variety of individuals. Few people could name more than six or seven towns. Many company towns have long disappeared, leaving little if any trace as time and nature have combined to erase their memory. A further complication is the fact that many people knowledgeable in their fields were not certain whether some towns were company-owned or not, and each town had to be checked out thoroughly.

Official company records would seem to be the best source of information, but several problems complicate the use of such material. First, in large corporations the records pertaining to the operation of the company town are integrated with a complicated mass of documents which may be made meaningful only through the long and painstaking efforts of a professional auditor or accountant. Such records, furthermore, reveal very little of the personal and social aspects of the company town which are important to this study. Finally, corporation documents are seldom available for use, not only because corporation policy often forbids such records being made a matter of public information, but also because many records pertaining to company towns have been lost or destroyed.

So little work has been done on the story of company towns that state historical societies generally are ignorant of such towns which may have existed within their states. Clipping files, however, are sometimes useful if one knows the name of a company or town to be studied. Company periodicals and histories are also helpful, and many are readily available. Departments of the federal government have studied certain social aspects and published the results in brief articles. These also have proved useful.

The most fruitful source of information has been correspondence and interviews with people who have lived in company towns. The scores of questionnaires and letters of inquiry sent out received approximately 75 per cent response. Seven of the eleven western states were toured, and dozens of former company-town residents, representing a fair cross section of management and labor personnel, were interviewed.

The Company-Town Image

A word must be said about the image of the company town. It seems almost axiomatic that company ownership and control was used to oppress employee-residents both economically and politically. "I owe my soul to the company store" is the familiar expression which flashes into the minds of many whenever the term "company town" is mentioned. The idea is often expressed that the company store was used as a tool for exploiting the worker by requiring him, as a condition of employment, to purchase all his goods through the store, and then charging exorbitantly high prices and actually encouraging perpetual debt to the company through credit buying and the scrip system. Under such a system, it is implied, the employee was little more than a serf, tied to company property not only through the need for work but also through his perpetual debt. Frequently mentioned, also, is the idea that managers could use their great dominance in the town to control voting and other political activity.

While there is apparently much substance to these charges, it is also obvious that this is not the whole picture. On the contrary, owners of many company towns actually had the interests of their employees at heart in the operation of company houses, company stores, and other economic activities. High prices in company stores were often caused by the increased cost involved in transporting goods to isolated areas. Some companies, however, such as Phelps Dodge Corporation, early established a rebate system whereby employees who traded in company stores shared in the profits, and no economic advantage actually accrued to the company by virtue simply of its store operation. The landlord company in many cases actually allowed competing stores to operate in the town, a few examples of which are cited in the text. In the matter of housing and community facilities, it is true that many companies provided only minimal quarters, concerning themselves very little with community planning, sanitary facilities, etc., but other companies took the responsibility of building comfortable homes, good community facilities, and churches. They seemed generally interested in creating a congenial atmosphere for the employees. The idea sometimes expressed that company paternalism was a factor in creating complacency and lack of ambition is demonstrated to be erroneous in many cases by the fact that employees frequently co-operated with the company in matters of community betterment, recreation organizations, etc., and that residents frequently took pride in creating attractive homes and yards and keeping their houses in repair.

In short, there is no general image applicable to all company towns. In some towns serious abuses of power occurred, while in others sincere and commendable efforts at company-employee co-operation were made. In some cases employees hated the managers, living for the day when they could get out of the town. In other instances the workers were highly satisfied and even disliked leaving at the termination of their employment. The positive side of company-town living will receive extra emphasis in the following pages in an effort to counteract the almost universal negative image which seems to exist.

Opportunities for Further Study

While this study is a pioneer effort at consolidating the story of the company town in the Far West, it is nevertheless general, and hopefully will suggest ideas for further fruitful research. A study of the company town in other large regions would be of significant value in testing the validity of some of the generalizations made here. A thorough study of the company towns of Hawaii, with this state's special economic and ethnic factors, would undoubtedly present some interesting problems entirely different in nature from those discussed here. Articles on the political or economic role of the company town in the development of particular states would also be of interest. In short, this study is intended as a first step in putting the story of the company-owned town in perspective with other types of communities which have characterized the evolution of America.

Organization

A brief explanation of the organization of this book seems appropriate. Company towns in the West have been most significant in three industries: coal, copper, and lumber. A chapter is devoted to each for the benefit of individuals interested in the over-all story of these particular industries. Another chapter is devoted to a brief survey of company towns in a variety of businesses. In these chapters detailed consideration has not been given to the numerous social, economic and political problems connected with company towns, except where a situation was peculiar to the particular industry involved. These themes have been left for separate chapters. The reader who is interested in the story of the company town in a particular industry, therefore, is advised not to stop with that chapter but to read also the chapters comprising the last half of the book, for several references will be made to particular towns in which he may have an interest.

JAMES B. ALLEN

Provo, Utah
February 24, 1966

Acknowledgments

GRATEFUL RECOGNITION is given Professor Donald C. Cutter, formerly of the University of Southern California and now at the University of New Mexico, who spent many hours reading the original manuscript of this work and making suggestions for improvement. Thanks are given also to Professor Joseph Boskin and Professor Totton J. Andersen, both of the University of Southern California, for reading the original study, and to Professor Eugene E. Campbell, of Brigham Young University, for reading the revised manuscript. To Professor Thomas G. Alexander, my colleague in Brigham Young University, I owe a special debt of gratitude for his preparation of the index during my absence from the United States. I further express appreciation for the many devoted hours spent by my wife, Renée J. Allen, in assisting with research problems, typing the manuscript, and proofreading. Grateful acknowledgment is extended to the following individuals and organizations who have furthered the research and publication of this book: Brigham Young University, Phelps Dodge Corporation, Mr. Gerald H. Galbreath, Jr., and Mr. Grant Taggart.

JAMES B. ALLEN

Contents

Illustrations

THE COMPANY TOWN IN THE AMERICAN WEST

A visitor in the historic Puget Sound region looking for the original site of old Fort Nisqually, built by the Hudson's Bay Company in 1833, would find himself in an attractive forest of Douglas firs near a small lake. Suddenly he would emerge into an attractive little village of approximately four hundred population. This is the town of DuPont which, from 1906 to 1950, was wholly owned and operated by E. I. Du Pont de Nemours and Company for the benefit of employees working at the company's powder plant. Near the Ammonium Nitrate Storage Building the visitor would find a bronze tablet marking the original location of Fort Nisqually.

The community of DuPont is of special interest for reasons other than its historic location. The neat wooden homes, all of similar architectural design, the isolated location, the now abandoned community hall, the rectangular layout, and the obvious domination of the town by one company are all marks of the typical company town in the American West. Perhaps hundreds of similar tiny communities, all owned outright by particular companies, have come and gone in the Western states. These towns have been created to support a variety of industries. DuPont belonged to a powder company. More common were scores of lumber communities which have dotted the forests of the Northwest, as well as those of California and Idaho. Coal-mining companies in Colorado, Utah, and New Mexico have built and operated many towns, and copper mining has contributed such towns to the states of Montana, Utah, Arizona, and New Mexico. Companies mining for other metals have also established communities. Near historic Leadville, Colorado, is the site of what was formerly one of the largest company towns in the West, Climax, which was called into being in the 1920's by the mining of molybdenum. Oil companies, cement manufacturers, potash and chemical manufacturers, and even cotton producers have all found occasion to build and operate, in different parts of the West, various company-owned towns.

Some Problems of Definition

What is a company town? At first glance, it might be defined simply as any community which has been built wholly to support the operations of a single company, in which all homes, buildings, and other real-estate property are owned by that company, having been acquired or erected specifically for the benefit of its employees, and in which the company provides most public services. Vast differences in the nearly two hundred communities studied, however, make necessary a few clarifications.

The company towns of Phelps Dodge Corporation disclose a wide range of conditions which modify the definition. The town of Morenci, Arizona, conforms closely to our definition. Owned outright by Phelps Dodge are all homes, business buildings, and public utilities, and a company store dominates the business life of the town. Private businesses exist, but their premises are leased from the company, which allows only those firms it considers necessary to the community. At the other end of the scale is Bisbee, Arizona. Life in Bisbee is almost wholly sustained by Phelps Dodge operations, and the company store is the dominant business. The company, furthermore, maintains a library in a company-owned building which also houses the post office. All the land in Bisbee is owned by the company, but the homes are almost all privately owned. Home owners lease their lots from the company at the token rate of one dollar a year. Many business firms compete directly with the company store, and Bisbee has its own city government, police force, chamber of commerce, and public utilities, all

4

acting independently of the company. The existence of private home ownership and self-government and the dominance of independent business firms places Bisbee outside our definition, and communities such as Bisbee have received only brief consideration here.

Two examples of towns often referred to as company towns but which are not typical of those included in this study are Douglas and Jerome, Arizona.[1] The latter, now abandoned, was one of the West's most unusual mining camps, and has achieved national fame. The town, however, was not a company-owned community. Residents owned their own land and homes. The town was incorporated, and it controlled its own government and public utilities. Douglas, Arizona, was founded in 1901 by James Douglas, of Phelps Dodge. Douglas and his associates formed the International Land and Improvement Company, acquiring all the property in Douglas and selling it as a profit-making venture to private home owners and businessmen. It seems apparent that such a settlement should not be included within the definition of a company town, even though company operations almost wholly sustain the life of the town.

Ajo, Arizona, is somewhere between the two extremes just discussed as far as company control is concerned. Here the company owns about one-half the land upon which residences and other buildings are located. The downtown plaza is owned by the company, but certain businessmen are allowed to lease the buildings according to company stipulations. Homes not located on company property are privately owned, and there are a number of private motels, restaurants, and other business facilities. Housing in the company section is completely controlled by Phelps Dodge, but no company control exists over the other half of the town. Com-

1 For the history of Jerome, see J. Carl Brogdon, "The History of Jerome, Arizona" (unpublished Master's thesis, Department of History, University of Arizona, 1952). For the story of Douglas, see Robert S. Jeffrey, "The History of Douglas, Arizona" (unpublished Master's thesis, Department of History, University of Arizona, 1951). Another interesting example of this kind of town is Longview, Wash. For its story, see John B. McClelland, Jr., *Longview . . . The Remarkable Beginnings of a Modern Western City.*

5

pany ownership of such a large portion of the town, however, compels its inclusion within our definition of a company town.

These variations make a simple definition of the company town impossible. For our purposes, however, the company town will be defined simply as any community which is owned and controlled by a particular company. The several modifications will serve to add interest and significance to the story.

Significance of the Company Town

The company town is not, of course, peculiar to the United States. In mining, for example, the very nature of the industry often compels the erection of company towns in remote sections of the world. One recent study of economic problems in the mineral industries reported:

> A problem of particular concern to the mining industry is raised by the relative remoteness verging on actual inaccessibility of many mining regions. The construction of industrial villages or towns is familiar to many industries and may be governed by access to labor, market, or raw material; but in few if any other industries is the locale so likely to be in underpopulated regions as in mining. Examples are the copper and other base-metal deposits of the Belgian Congo and the Andes of Chile and Peru, the tin mining regions of Bolivia, the cryolite mining centers in Greenland, the Alpine villages surrounding the lead-zinc deposits of northern Italy and Austria, and the mining towns on the Arctic Circle in the iron districts of northern Sweden. These locations, far from other pre-existing population centers, compel the construction of whole villages or towns, with their schools, hospitals, water supply, and food depots, replete with roads, railroads, and landing fields. Even in the United States this may be necessary where a large ore deposit in a new area is being opened.[2]

The significance of the company town in the American West is seen partly in the almost unanimous response from management to

2 Charles A. Beher, Jr., and Nathaniel Arbiter, "Distinctive Features of the Mineral Industries," in Edward H. Robie (ed.), *Economics of the Mineral Industries: A Series of Articles by Specialists*, 75–76.

6

two questions: "Why did the company town come into existence?" and, "Why are company towns so rapidly disappearing from the scene?" Almost invariably the answer to the first question is that the company town was an economic necessity to the company involved. Mining companies establishing themselves in isolated areas often found it necessary to provide housing for workers in order to get them to come. The company, furthermore, could not sell lots, for the land might some day prove worth developing. All this led to a need for the company to provide a system of community regulation as well as facilities for recreation, medical care, and all other services required in any residential area. Lumber companies, too, often set up operations in remote forest areas so removed from civilization that it would have been impractical for men to commute, even on weekends. The company town, therefore, became especially significant in the successful expansion of the mining and lumber industries of the West.

The answer to the second query, "Why are company towns so rapidly disappearing from the scene?" serves to emphasize the significance of the first. Depleted ore and timber supplies have eliminated many towns. Others, however, simply have been sold to employees as management has become convinced that company ownership is no longer needed. Modern highways, automobiles, and other developments in transportation have brought the communities of the West much closer together. No longer are even the more isolated villages so far from civilization that the company is compelled to provide stores, churches, and other necessities of community life. Many companies are frank to admit that company towns are an economic burden which they would gladly relinquish. Some companies, such as Phelps Dodge Corporation, see good economic reasons for maintaining basic control of their communities. Other companies, such as American Smelting and Refining Company, which owns the little town of Silver Bell, Arizona, still operate in very remote areas and expect their operations to be of a temporary nature. Here the company-owned town is still considered essential. Except for a few isolated cases, however, the company town is slowly being eliminated from the Western American scene.

In short, the gradual disappearance of the company town is but a part of the dramatic economic evolution of the nation. As economic necessity compelled its origin, so economic considerations demand its eventual absorbtion into the main stream of American community life. Herein lies the story of the company town as a feature of Western American development.

CHAPTER I

Early Company Towns

ALTHOUGH DEVELOPMENT of a company town was usually the result of a conscious effort on the part of the company, many early mining and lumbering communities simply grew haphazardly at the sites of new mines or mills. Simple workmen's shanties would be scattered here and there on company property, although frequently the company would build additional housing facilities. Most early mining camps could not be called company towns, for no single firm owned all the property or provided housing and other facilities, but a few such communities came to be wholly dominated by a single company and might legitimately be considered early versions of the Western company town.

One such camp was Tubac, in southern Arizona (then part of New Mexico Territory). In 1856 the Sonora Exploring and Mining Company was organized in New York, with Major S. P. Heintzelman as president and Charles D. Poston as "Commandant and Managing agent." Convinced that the Gadsden Purchase region was rich in mineral wealth, Poston headed a group which set out to open mines in the area. Tubac, a presidio originally established by the Spaniards on the Santa Rita River, had been abandoned by Mexican troops because of the hostile Apache Indians in the area. Poston's company took over and began to repair the settlement, soon preparing accommodations for three hundred men. Mexican workers flocked to the new mines, called the Heintzelman mines, and others re-occupied abandoned farms in the area. Poston became almost a country baron, presiding over the entire valley as well as the presidio. He opened a book of

9

records, performed marriages, baptized children, and granted divorces. He records that such authority was not always looked upon with favor by all concerned:

> By the way, I narrowly escaped getting into trouble with the church. I had been marrying and divorcing, baptizing children and granting absolution as Alcalde of Tubac but the vicar said that would never do. He refused to recognize my legal marriages according to the laws of Mexico, and insisted on the rights of the church.
>
> The domestic situation on the Santa Cruz bordered on rebellion, and the only way out of the dilemma was to advance the disconsolate husbands nearly a thousand dollars to pay for the sanction of the church on their matrimonial ventures, and to have their Carlos' and Carlottas baptized with Holy Water instead of Whiskey.[1]

Although a company store apparently was not operated at Tubac, the company dominated the economic life of its workers. It provided lodging for those who stayed at the presidio, and it paid its workers in "boletas," or scrip issued by the company and accepted by the merchants. This strange money was made of cardboard about two and one-half inches by four inches in size on which were printed pictures of animals (apparently to help illiterate Mexican workers identify its value). The various denominations were: 12.5 cents (a pig); 25 cents (a calf); 50 cents (a rooster); one dollar (a horse); five dollars (a bull); and ten dollars (a lion).

Tubac showed every sign of continuing prosperity, but in 1861 renewed Apache attacks forced its abandonment.[2] Perhaps the settlement would not have evolved into a full-fledged company town, but its story is significant here as an example of early

---

1 Charles D. Poston, MS of a speech apparently delivered in 1896, typewritten copy on file at the Pioneer Historical Society of Arizona, Tucson.

2 For more on Tubac, see A. W. Gressinger, *Charles D. Poston, Sunland Seer*, 22–35; Bernice Cosulich, "When Old Tubac was Young and Prosperous," *Arizona Daily Star*, February 21, 1932.

10

tendencies toward complete single-company control of mining communities in the West.

It was not uncommon for a little community to spring up haphazardly around specific mining areas on property owned by the company. A motley assortment of privately owned shacks would appear, and a store would come into operation, but the company would control the town, such as it was. Such a settlement was Helvetia, in Arizona, which flourished around the turn of the century. Its shacks were described by a contemporary as "not much of a thing and made of bear grass."[3] While the company did not completely regulate the town, it did have enough interest to make an agreement with the county superintendent of schools to erect a schoolhouse. Thus Helvetia might be considered an early camp with a few of the markings of the company town.[4]

Morenci, Arizona, is an example of a flourishing copper-mining camp which eventually evolved into a full-blown company town. The area was settled in 1872 by William Church, of the Detroit Copper Mining Company, and was first called Joy's Camp. Church developed the mining claims and in 1880 began construction of a mill and several buildings in the adjoining settlement of Clifton. Here he also constructed a combination store and boardinghouse as well as two cottages for himself and his brother.

Clifton did not become a company town, but after the Detroit Copper Mining Company was taken over by Phelps Dodge Corporation in 1897, Morenci eventually came under complete company control. At this time, however, Morenci represented the typical rough-and-tumble mining camp. The residential section, called "Old Town" by the ladies but dubbed "Hell Town" by everyone else, consisted of dwellings thrown together with adobe, tin cans, dry-goods boxes, barrel staves, and almost anything else which could be held together with nails or plaster. The business

3 José del Castillo, MS collection on Arizona, filed at the library of the Pioneer Historical Society of Arizona, Tucson. From interview with Joe Kirby by José del Castillo, March 4 and 7, 1939.

4 *The Arizona Republican*, January 13, 1900.

section was composed mainly of saloons, dance halls, and gambling houses, all of which were forbidden in most genuine company towns. One resident described early Morceni this way:

> You see Morenci as I recall it was the Morenci of about forty years ago—a crude Spanish-speaking community with two Mexican settlements—with few whites, the one big company store—the only level stretch where a boy and girl could go walking was a short piece of railroad grade leading to the cemetery—and the white Spaniards bought a keg of wine—laid it across the railroad track and rolled it on the track around the spurs to their shacks. Before that—in the ten years preceding 1900—Morenci and Tombstone were called the toughest wildest mining camps in the west—and it was said one could step out any morning and see a corpse down at the foot of the dump. Even while I was there—shootings, knifings, and brawls were common occurrences. . . .[5]

Shortly after the acquisition by Phelps Dodge, fire destroyed "Old Town," and a new townsite was graded by the company. A new company store was built in 1901, a hotel was soon completed, and the Morceni Club was erected for the use of company employees. The Morceni Water Company was organized to bring more water to the town, and the Morenci Improvement Company was established to build houses. The rough-and-tumble mining community of the old Detroit Copper Mining Company had thus evolved into an authentic company town.

While Tubac was beginning to prosper in the Southwest, the lumber industry was beginning to thrive in the Northwest. In 1853 the first lumber company town to be built in the West was founded at Port Gamble, Washington Territory, by the Puget Mill Company. This picturesque and comfortable mill town was well planned from the beginning, patterned faithfully after the typical New England town. Scotia, California, on the other hand, although

---

[5] Roberta Watt, "History of Morenci, Arizona" (unpublished Master's thesis, Department of History, University of Arizona, 1956), 136. Quoting a letter written by John M. Boutwell.

12

a model company town today, began as a rustic forest camp with cabins built wherever there was a clearing. Street alignment came much later, about 1915, when the company moved some of the cabins and got rid of the "sawtooth route" through town.[6] As with Port Gamble, Scotia was a company town from its inception, but it took a period of evolution for it to develop from a forest camp to a well-planned town.

In coal mining, Sunnyside, Utah, stands as a good example of a haphazard mining camp which eventually developed into a typical company town. Coal was discovered there about 1880, and production began in the 1890's. The first buildings in the area were privately owned, but when Utah Fuel Company acquired title to the immense tract of land, it demanded that all settlers move. The company began to erect houses but could not keep up with the fast growing population. Many residents, therefore, built their own homes, which the company later purchased. In addition, many put up tents in the southern part of the canyon, and this section became known as "Rag Town" by local residents. Company-owned houses were hastily erected frame structures, not plastered inside, but about 1915 the company began a program of building better homes and modernizing the town.[7]

This brief review of a few early company towns of the West simply illustrates the variety of ways in which company towns developed. In the following chapters the company town will be discussed in connection with specific industries, thus giving a clearer picture of the role played by this institution in the economic development of the West.

[6] Interview with Alden Ball, public relations representative, Pacific Lumber Co., Scotia, Calif., April 18, 1962.

[7] Lucille Richins, "A Social History of Sunnyside" (Utah Historical Records Survey, March, 1940, MS filed at the Utah State Historical Society, Salt Lake City), 2–3.

CHAPTER II

The Lumber Industry

A REVIEW OF COMPANY TOWNS established in the forests of Western America does not give a complete picture of the development of the lumber industry, for not every major lumber manufacturer found it necessary or desirable to go to the expense of building and operating such communities. Some companies located their mills near well-rooted centers of population, thus simply contributing to the growth of economies already established. On the other hand, many lumber companies found it to their advantage to go into the paternalism of company-town ownership. A review of some of these will prove valuable in two respects: (a) it will demonstrate the significance of the company town in a major portion of the lumber industry, and (b) it will demonstrate certain economic changes which have affected not only the towns themselves but also the entire industry. Lumber has played an important role in the economies of Oregon, California, Washington, Idaho, and Montana, and it is in these five states that most lumber company-owned towns of the West have been located.

Logging Camps

Most company towns in the lumber industry were established in connection with sawmills, but housing and other facilities were also provided for logging crews. Logging camps did not generally become towns, for the nature of logging itself demanded that crews keep moving to new cutting areas. Practically every large lumber company provided cook houses, bunkhouses, and a commissary for its logging crews. Many shacks were built so that

14

wheels could be attached for easy movement to new locations, and others were built on skids. Cabins were even constructed as barges and simply floated down the river at moving time. For the most part these were not family camps but only temporary quarters for the logger, whose family, if he had one, was living in a nearby non-company town.

A few of these transient settlements, however, were also family camps and were even classed as towns. Shevlin, Oregon, owned by the Shevlin-Hixon Company, had a post office, and it received wide publicity because of its frequent shifts from one location to another. The postal service was finally discontinued on April 1, 1951.[1]

A few logging camps became permanent company-owned towns. In northern California, for example, the town of Tennant was established by the Weed Lumber Company in 1921. In addition to family residences it had rooming houses, a store, barbershop, church, and theater. Steam heat and electric lights were also provided in the community, which continued to operate as a logging headquarters until 1950, when the entire town was donated to the Veterans of Foreign Wars.

A Company-Owned Mill Town

On December 1, 1849, Andrew Jackson Pope and Frederic Talbot, young business adventurers from East Machias, Maine, landed at the little settlement of San Francisco, California. The new city was just beginning to grow, and Pope and Talbot were determined to grow with it. By January they had gone into the lumber business under the name of Pope and Talbot, selling lumber purchased from sailing vessels. The dense forests of the West Coast were still virtually untapped, and most of San Francisco's lumber came, not cheaply, from the East. In March, 1849, for example, Captain William C. Talbot, Frederic's brother, arrived from Maine with his brig, the *Oriental*, loaded with sixty thousand feet of lumber, two house-frames, an assortment of joists and timbers,

1 Lewis A. McArthur, *Oregon Geographic Names*, 547.

15

and a few shingles. The Talbot brothers, Pope, and Captain J. P. Keller were soon operating a business which included trips of the *Oriental* to the islands, lighterage operations, and sporadic lumber sales.[2]

Lumber shipped from the East, however, was obviously too expensive to rely upon permanently, especially when good lumber was available from the virgin forests of the Northwest. Pope and Talbot became interested in tapping these reserves. Since they wanted to ship as well as manufacture lumber, their proposed sawmill had to be located at tidewater at a point where sailing vessels would have good anchorage and a safe harbor. Thus they decided to build their mill somewhere on Puget Sound. Such considerations are significant here, for the same factors led to the creation of several company towns along the Pacific Coast. Early lumber manufacturers owned and operated not only the mill, but also the harbor and ships by which their products could be transported to San Francisco.

On November 29, 1851, A. J. Pope, W. C. Talbot, and J. P. Keller formed the Puget Mill Company, a subsidiary of Pope and Talbot. In the summer of 1853 Captain Talbot sailed into the densely wooded Strait of Juan de Fuca on his search for an adequate coastal millsite. Included in his cargo were a few thousand feet of Eastern boards for use in constructing a cabin and cook house for his men to use while the new sawmill was being built. He finally located a small peninsula in a sheltered bay about five miles from the entrance of Hood Canal. Here was a level, sandy spit, perfect for a mill, and stands of timber grew near the water's edge. The settlement that Talbot founded here was called Teekalet until the 1860's, when the name was changed to Port Gamble.

By September the mill frame was up, and in that month Keller arrived in the schooner *L. P. Foster*. He brought with him an

2 Edwin T. Coman, Jr., and Helen Gibbs, *Time, Tide and Timber: A Century of Pope and Talbot, passim.* Most of the information on Port Gamble is taken from this source.

engine, boilers, mill machinery, merchandise for the store, and other supplies essential to the life of the infant company town. He also brought his wife and one of his daughters, who became the first white women at Port Gamble. The project was rapidly successful, and soon cargo was being shipped from Puget Sound to San Francisco, and thence to various parts of the world. The Puget Mill Company quickly developed a trade larger than that of any other mill on the Sound, and it weathered well the periods of overproduction and depression which occasionally struck the thriving West Coast lumber industry.

In 1858 a second mill was constructed at Port Gamble, bringing in thirty-two new mill hands. The expanded operations called for more help in the company store (which served not only Port Gamble but also surrounding settlements), machine shop, and blacksmith shop. The company also furnished "choppers" and teamsters to the loggers who had contracted to furnish the mill with logs, hence the need for many additional workmen.

Common labor at the mills was often performed by Indians, who were found to be competent workers. As their number grew, the company built a village for them, called Little Boston, across Gamble Bay. It became common in company towns to provide separate villages or separate sections of town for non-white races, usually because each race simply preferred to live separately and carry out its own social customs without disturbance.

For a time Port Gamble was the most prominent settlement in the region. Coman and Gibbs give the following description of its significance and early activities:

> Near-by settlements also furnished recruits, men who were in need of a cash income, some of them temporarily. During the Indian scare, dozens of people in Seattle went over to Port Gamble. Yesler's mill had been forced to close, and Seattle got a setback from which it did not recover for years. . . . Fred Drew, who had just arrived at Port Gamble, later recorded this terse description of what the immediate vicinity was like in 1858:

17

"When the steamboat 'Brother Jonathan' landed at Victoria in April, 1858, the only building there outside of the Hudson Bay Company stockade was a partly finished hotel.

"At that time Whatcom was a small coal mine—Port Townsend a collection of saloons and sailor boarding houses. . . . Port Gamble was a saw mill of 25 M (thousand) twelve hour daily capacity —Seattle a hamlet containing ninety odd white inhabitants."

Small wonder that men, especially those with families, were attracted to the thriving mill town of Port Gamble. The mills and related operations offered employment for more than 175 men, and those who were married lived in neat little frame houses that the company had built. The store carried the largest stock on the Sound and did a cash business of $50 a day. A. J. Pope, who did most of the buying, each month sent up goods and supplies valued at from $15,000 to $20,000 for the store and mill at Port Gamble.

At Port Gamble a man could be sure of $30 a month for an 11½-hour day that started at six in the morning and ended twelve hours later. He could also be sure of a roof over his head and hot meals. As a result, the mill whistle at twenty minutes past five in the morning served as an alarm clock for several men who later became prominent on Puget Sound.[3]

As the company expanded it absorbed other mills in the area. In 1878 the Port Ludlow Mill Company was purchased, although operations were not opened there for another five years. Port Ludlow was located at the head of Hood Canal, and after 1884 it became another flourishing company town.

Port Gamble was unique among company towns. Conceived and nurtured by State-of-Mainers, it took on a New England atmosphere. The orderly layout and the trim, white company-built houses resembled almost exactly a New England village. Many of the homes were well furnished, including many antiques, and by the 1880's all houses had running water. The company-built church was a replica of the Congregational church at East Machias,

3 *Ibid.*, 69–70.

Maine. Port Gamble is still company owned, although some of the old homes have been eliminated, and some new subdivisions are being developed for sale. The picturesque main street, however, lined with shade trees and the better New England-style homes, will be preserved by the company as a landmark.[4]

In most company towns the almost exalted status of the resident manager was dramatically illustrated by the more commodious and sometimes ostentatious house built for him. At Port Gamble, Cyrus Walker had the finest home in town. When it burned in 1885, Walker decided to rebuild at Port Ludlow, and the spacious mansion which was completed in 1887 was called Admiralty Hall. It was built of the finest lumber available, and the huge front doors resembled those of a ship's cabin. The elegant furniture included pieces made of black walnut shipped from Maine and a massive sideboard made in Dresden about 1750. The house was strategically located on a rolling slope overlooking Ludlow Bay. A cannon mounted on the front lawn was used to fire salutes to ships entering the bay, as well as an annual Fourth of July sunrise salute. Few company towns could boast of a mansion as imposing as Admiralty Hall.

Cyrus Walker had complete control of most of the town. A teetotaler, he did not favor the sale of liquor, though he allowed it to be sold at the company store. The biggest problem, however, was in the hotel, which was not owned by the company. Here alcohol flowed freely, and drinking, together with weekend poker parties, often made mill hands late for work. The company finally purchased the hotel in order to control it. Walker also concerned himself about other threats to the morals of his town, refusing to permit women of "questionable character" to enter company property. Such activities as they might have engaged in, however, could not be completely controlled, for it was a common sight to see "a string of rowboats making their way across Gamble Bay, filled with

4 Interview with Cyrus T. Walker, vice-president, Pope & Talbot, Inc., Portland, Ore., April 26, 1962.

19

sailors intent on appraising the charms of the squaws of Little Boston."[5]

Port Gamble and Port Ludlow are representative of many company towns in the lumber industry. Located at harbors because of the need to provide shipping as well as cutting facilities, they grew as the number of company employees increased. That their stable population came largely from the state of Maine symbolizes the westward jump taken by the Maine-born American lumber industry. Eighty-six million feet of lumber issued from the sawmills in Port Gamble and Port Ludlow in the year 1901, and company-owned vessels carried cargoes to all parts of the world. In the sense that the company town was an important part of the growing lumber industry of the West, it was indeed significant.

Town with a Different History

In 1857 the Washington Mill Company began to produce lumber at Seabeck, farther up Hood Canal. The history of Seabeck presents quite a different picture from that of Port Gamble and serves to illustrate the differences which may exist between company towns.[6]

Under its first resident manager, Marshall Blinn, Seabeck seemed to prosper. Even Edward Clayson, who became the company's most vocal critic, was glowing in his praise of the town's earliest days. Clayson, one of the principal loggers on the Sound, owned property just outside the town, built a small hotel, and operated his own little sloop up and down the Sound. Describing the robust early days of Seabeck, he said:

> We had a good library at Seabeck, a Sunday School, a brass band, two hotels, three saloons, a baseball ground at Clayson's; the common school ran six months in the year; a traveling show would

[5] Coman and Gibbs, *Time, Tide and Timber*, 172.

[6] Seabeck story based on Edward Clayson, Sr., *Historical Narrative of Puget Sound, Hoods Canal, 1865–1885: The Experiences of an Only Free Man in a Penal Colony;* Judith M. Johnson, "Some Materials for Pacific Northwest History. Washington Mill Company Papers," *Pacific Northwest Quarterly*, Vol. V (July, 1960); and E. E. Riddell, "History of Seabeck," mimeographed MS (revised, 1952).

come along two or three times a year, and a preacher about once a month. Fourth of July or Christmas and election days were "events" that were always full of life; in our little metropolis at Seabeck we had about sixteen families, and as fine and robust a lot of healthy children as could be found.[7]

In 1870 Richard Holyoke was appointed mill superintendent. Holyoke was entirely different from Blinn, and under him Washington Mill Company began to lose the respect and prestige it had previously enjoyed. Other companies made competition more difficult by offering the loggers higher wages, and the Washington Mill Company began to lose ground.[8] Edward Clayson began to regard Holyoke as a tyrant ruling the company town of Seabeck like a penal colony. Clayson published a little newspaper called the *Rebel Battery*, with the avowed purpose of waging war on Washington Mill Company. In later years he published his memoirs, and some excerpts will illustrate the extremes to which people have gone in criticizing companies that owned and controlled their own communities:

> In that penal colony—Seabeck—was a public bridge, built with the public funds. . . . This bridge crossed a creek about 200 feet wide, connecting this "penal colony" with rebel territory (this lonely rebel rebelled against the King of Hoods Canal). This territory comprised some 133 acres of land, with 450 yards of waterfront, and it belonged to Edward Clayson. . . .
>
> For many long years there was never a school meeting in Seabeck—there was the form of a meeting, that's all. The "formality" had to be complied with . . . in order to get the annual appropriation of school money for the payment of the teachers.
>
> A notice of the annual school meeting, as required by law, was always stuck up on the outside of the Washington Mill Company's store, and just enough of Holly-Hawke's "subjects" used to assemble in the company's hall every year to form a "school com-

---

7 Clayson, *Historical Narrative of Puget Sound,* 5.
8 Johnson, "Some Materials for Pacific Northwest History. Washington Mill Company Papers," *Pacific Northwest Quarterly,* Vol. V (July, 1960), 136–38.

mittee." One "subject" would make a motion and another "subject" would second it. The motion was put to an empty hall, and the motion always carried unanimously to an empty school house. What a damn mockery to be sure! In 1878 or 1879 . . . there was a school meeting for the first time in the twenty years' history of Seabeck, and it was a "violent demonstration, too," being as it was that of a "foreign born citizen" championing (single handed and alone) "free speech"; and the "loil subjects" —native born American slaves—opposing it. . . .

This shows to what depths of degredation a community can be reduced to in isolated parts of the country under corporate dominion and the despotic rule of a local agent of an "absentee landlord."[9]

Whatever the truth may have been, Seabeck remained under company control until 1886, when the mill burned. It was never rebuilt, and the employees scattered to other mills in the area.

The Short-Lived Mill Town

The lumber industry frequently has been criticized for its early practice of going into an area of virgin timber, establishing a mill, and wantonly cutting out an entire area. Much timber was wasted when only the choice trees and the choice parts of trees were milled, the rest being burned or left to rot. As soon as an area was "cut out" lumbermen would move on to new stands of timber, abandoning many mill settlements. Most were completely deserted, although remnants of others may still exist as small settlements supporting farming communities. In Mendocino County, California, for example, the tiny settlement of Navarro was once a small, company-owned community called Wendling, but today only a few ranches and an Italian café mark the area.

A good example of the short-lived mill town which flourished in the early part of this century was Montezuma, Washington. Montezuma was a full-fledged company town with bunkhouses, cottages, a company store, recreation hall, and a population of five or six

9 Clayson, *Historical Narrative of Puget Sound*, 27–28, 46.

hundred people. It supported the mill operations of the Manley-Moore Lumber Company from 1910 to 1935. Typically, the town was established because of transportation difficulties. Only a logging railroad led into the area, and there was no way of transporting men daily from any other town. "We needed employees for our operations and we had to build places for them to live and provide the necessary services for them," reported the company's superintendent.[10] In addition to the mill town, Manley-Moore also had many of the usual mobile logging camps in the woods.

Montezuma was typical of most small company towns in the lumber region. A cottage could be rented for eight dollars a month. Lights were free, and fuel wood could be purchased from the company for seventy-five cents a cord. At the company store employees were allowed to have their purchases deducted from the payroll, though no effort was made to force them to trade in the company store. Some employees purchased goods at a nearby mining camp. When the mill was closed in 1935, the town was soon abandoned.

Economic Changes Affect Company Towns

Although the frequent disbanding of sawmills and the abandonment of adjacent communities have led to the bringing of charges of waste and poor management against the lumber industry, there have been some compelling reasons for the moves. A 1946 study of the abandonment of mill towns in the Puget Sound region reached some interesting conclusions.[11] The forest industry, stated the author, began with a pioneer exploitation stage which could not have been different because of conditions existing at the time. Intensive competition, the expense of salvaging poor quality timber, the profuseness of the forests, the lack of modern salvaging and utilization techniques, and the lack of public concern over scientific forest practices all worked together to cause the period of exploita-

10 Interview with Mr. R. R. Roberts, of Portland, Ore., May 29, 1962.

11 Clark Irwin Cross, "Factors Influencing the Abandonment of Lumber Mill Towns in the Puget Sound Region" (unpublished Master's thesis, School of Forestry, University of Oregon, 1946), *passim.*

tion. The early economy lacked population, transportation, local markets, and settlements. Timber operators found it necessary to establish camps or company towns. In this pioneer stage the industry was designed to harvest only virgin timber, and the life of a small mill was very uncertain, dependent as it was upon a stand of timber soon to disappear. The author concluded that a "mature forest economy" had been reached by 1937–38, based on sustained-yield forest practices. That many towns have been abandoned and that no new ones are being built are signs of this maturity.

The conservation movement has had an important effect upon the lumber industry. By the 1920's trained foresters and members of Congress realized that the cutting of timber four times faster than it could replace itself would soon eliminate the industry. Under the prodding of William B. Greeley, chief forester in the Department of the Interior, Congress passed legislation in 1924 designed to encourage reforestation by private timber growers.[12] A federally supported fire-prevention program and certain tax incentives were used in encouraging reforestation, as well as a program of education designed to gain public support for the government's aims. The effect of conservation and reforestation is seen in the fact that in 1923 the annual cut of saw timber was four times greater than the yearly growth, but by 1946 the rate had decreased to only one and one-half times the annual reforestation.

The conservation movement has added new elements to the lumber industry. Large companies now hire trained foresters to plan and supervise permanent forest programs on company property. Large "tree farms" have sprung up in every part of the lumber region, as cut-over areas are reseeded by helicopter or replanted with seedlings grown in company nurseries. Cutting and other forest practices are scientifically planned to eliminate de-

12 For the vital and interesting story of Greeley's fight with Gifford Pinchot over the principle of private versus public control of commercial cutting, as well as Greeley's tireless efforts to persuade Congress to pass his conservation program, see George T. Morgan, Jr., *William B. Greeley, A Practical Forester, passim.*

24

struction of future commercial timber. New processing methods, new uses, and better marketing practices have given real commercial value to wood formerly wasted.

A dramatic illustration of the changing pattern of the lumber industry and its effect upon company towns is seen in the story of Rockport, California. This settlement on the Mendocino County coast began in the 1880's as a typical lumber camp. The mill was located near an inlet from the ocean so that timber could be shipped via company vessels to San Francisco. The town grew slowly as it passed through the hands of various owners, and in 1938 the present owner, Rockport Redwood Company, took over. When the sawmill shut down in 1957 the town's population was about five hundred. All the typical features of a company town were present at Rockport, including the company store, community hall, and company doctor. Today, however, practically all the houses are deserted, and Rockport is no longer a legitimate town. Rockport Redwood Company has become a timber supplier, and the Rockport area is now a giant tree farm. Also located here is a company nursery, and the mountains surrounding the former community are covered with an imposing new growth of redwood which in eighty to one hundred years will be sold for commercial milling. The rise and decline of the town of Rockport, therefore, uniquely demonstrates the evolution of the lumber industry, from the early days of a cutting and shipping operation to the present management of sustained-yield forests.

The changing pattern of the lumber industry has had quite a different effect upon the town of McCleary, Washington. McCleary had its beginning in 1898 as a sawmill and logging camp, and shortly after the turn of the century the operation was taken over by the Henry McCleary Timber Company, with Henry McCleary dominant owner and manager of the town. The world's largest fir-door plant, which stimulated the substantial growth of the town, opened in McCleary in 1912. In 1942 McCleary's timber resources were exhausted, and the company sold the mill, together

25

with the town, to the Simpson Logging Company, of Shelton, Washington. The Simpson company, however, had long been interested in sustained-yield forest practices and was already in the business of tree farming, practicing other methods of conservation as well. Simpson, moreover, was not interested in the problems of company-town ownership, and the company's policy of maintaining a permanent supply of timber made possible the assurance of a permanent economy at McCleary. The Simpson company therefore offered the town's homes for sale to its tenants at a price equivalent to eighteen months' rent, and McCleary became an incorporated, self-governing community. Simpson also improved the town's water and lighting systems, selling these utilities to the town for less than the cost of the improvements. In this case, changing forest economy has resulted in the evolution of a company town from a paternalistic "one-man" community to a self-governing, progressive community of home owners with a new lease on life and a bright new future.[13]

Along with changing forest practices another modern element has been introduced into the lumber industry: the consolidation and development of giant corporations. This might be considered a third factor in the process of the gradual elimination of company towns in the West. The Simpson Logging Company (now the Simpson Timber Company), for example, not only took over the McCleary operations but in 1956 also purchased the properties of the Northern Redwood Company at Korbel, California. Korbel was an old-time mill town founded in 1882 by the Korbel brothers. The Simpson company, following its policy of not becoming involved in town-management problems, began gradually to eliminate the company town. Residents were encouraged to purchase homes in nearby communities, and eventually company housing at Korbel will be eliminated entirely. Soon another company town will have passed into oblivion.

[13] An interesting account of McCleary's development is seen in *The McCleary Stimulator*, December 4, 1958. See also Stewart Holbrook, *Green Commonwealth*.

One of America's giant lumber firms is the Georgia-Pacific Corporation, which holds vast timber reserves in the West and Southeast, where the company originally began in 1927.[14] By 1960 the firm had taken over many smaller companies, and among the Western firms were Feather River Pine Mills Company, of Feather Falls, California, and Hammond Lumber Company, of Samoa, California, both of which owned company towns.

The development of such giant corporations in the lumber industry has had an influence upon company towns. The original founder of a mill town, in most cases, had a personal interest in the community. His company was small enough that he knew the people of the town, and if he did not live in the town he frequently visited it. With the modern trend toward consolidation, however, has come decreasing personal interest. As properties are acquired in widely separated areas, the president of a company has little to do directly with the residents of any town which may happen to be acquired in the consolidation process. It is not in their interest, furthermore, for the corporations to continue to provide services once offered in the company town, for the advancement of civilization has given easy access to these towns, and employees can commute from elsewhere. Existing housing may be sold to tenants, for the new security given by the long-term nature of the business promises continued life to the community. If the company town is retained, it is often used as a residential area for key personnel, with the majority of workers living in nearby communities. In short, the company town is nothing more than a passing detail when compared with the vast operations of some of today's huge enterprises. The towns have had their place in the development of the lumber industry but are only incidental to the corporations which are now acquiring them.

A case in point is Georgia-Pacific's take-over of Hammond Lumber Company in 1956. Two California company towns were

---

14 For an interesting and comprehensive account of Georgia-Pacific Corp. and its phenomenal growth, see John McDonald, "George Pacific: It Grows Big on Trees," *Fortune*, Vol. LXV, No. 5 (May, 1962).

affected by this transaction: Crannell and Samoa. Georgia-Pacific soon decided to eliminate the mill in Crannell as well as the town itself, and everything except a few of the newer houses was dismantled. One company town, therefore, was completely removed from the scene. Samoa, on the other hand, which was the center of the Hammond operations, was maintained, but with a changed atmosphere. A. B. Hammond, founder of Hammond Lumber Company, had taken a keen personal interest in the town and its people. Today, however, there seems to be little personal interest in the town as such on the part of top management, although company officials at the site who were once a part of the Hammond organization still take pride in the community. The town is maintained basically for key personnel, and low-cost housing is part of their incentive. A larger portion of the employees live out of town than in former years, and the company no longer maintains stores, the recreational hall, or other facilities characteristic of true company towns. Although no official policy tending toward elimination of the town has been announced, one who drives through the area today receives a definite, almost unexplainable feeling that Samoa is another company town that may not exist as such for many more years to come.[15]

Another corporation which has grown large in recent years through taking over smaller companies is the International Paper Company. In 1956 International Paper acquired all the holdings of the Long-Bell Lumber Company, including the company town of Weed, California. The new owner had no company towns of its own and took immediate steps to get rid of this one by selling company homes to its employees. International Paper Company still operates a large mill at Weed, but the few houses it still owns are maintained for key management personnel.

[15] It is not implied that Samoa is an unpleasant place to live, for the company-owned houses appear unusually comfortable and well built, and the town is well maintained. The lack of any normal "town" activities, however, the increasing closeness of other communities, and the fact there is no real need for the company to stay in the business of owning a town explain the feeling suggested above.

28

It would be difficult to say that consolidation of lumber interests universally leads to elimination of company towns, but the tendency seems to be in this direction. The same economic factors, at least, which have aided this consolidation trend have also contributed to a lessening need for company-owned communities in the lumber industry.

Towns Which Endure

Although no new company-owned towns are developing in the lumber industry, and the general trend is toward elimination of present towns, many long-time company towns which show no immediate prospects of being sold or eliminated still exist in the West. Reasons for continuing to operate the towns include: (1) company desire to retain firm control of the property adjoining its mills; (2) the still relatively isolated position of a few communities, which would tend to discourage a desire for home ownership; and (3) the fact that low-cost but desirable housing can be an added incentive in attracting personnel, especially in management positions.

In Washington, present-day company towns include only Port Gamble, owned by Pope and Talbot, Inc.; and Sappho, established as logging headquarters for Bloedell-Donovan in 1924 and now owned by Rayonier, Inc. Company towns in Oregon include: Gilchrist, established in 1938 by the Gilchrist Timber Company; Kinzua, founded in 1927 and owned by the Kinzua Corporation; Valsetz, established in 1919 and owned by the Valsetz Lumber Company; Vaughn, established in the 1920's and now owned by International Paper Company; Wauna, founded in 1912 by Wauna Lumber Company; and Westfir, founded about 1925 by Western Lumber Company and now owned by Edward Hines Lumber Company.

Some present-day California company towns are: Feather Falls, established in 1938 by the Feather Falls River Pine Mills Company and now owned by Georgia-Pacific; Hilt, founded about

29

1912 and owned by Fruit Growers Supply Company; Johnsondale, established in 1936–37 by Mt. Whitney Lumber Company, now a division of American Forest Products Corporation; Korbel, founded by Korbel brothers in the 1880's and now a part of Simpson Timber Company, although gradually being eliminated; McCloud, the property of the McCloud River Lumber Company since the 1890's, but transferred to United States Plywood Corporation in 1963 and, after 1965, gradually being sold to employees of that firm; Samoa, established in the 1890's by Vance Lumber Company and now a part of Georgia-Pacific; Scotia, the property of the Pacific Lumber Company since the 1880's; and Standard, established by the Standard Lumber Company in 1910 and now owned by Pickering Lumber Corporation.

In Arizona the town of McNary has been in operation by the McNary Lumber Company since 1935. The town of Bonner, Montana, was established in the 1880's by Hammond Lumber Company and is currently owned by the Anaconda Company's lumber department. In Idaho the community of Potlatch was founded in 1928 and is still the property of Potlatch Forests, Inc.

Of all the lumber company towns in the West, Scotia, California, has probably received the most publicity.[16] The history of Scotia began about 1885 when the Pacific Lumber Company built a railroad into Forestville, as Scotia then was known, and the following year constructed a mill. The settlement was located on a large bend of the Eel River. By 1888 the company was the top producer of redwood in Humboldt County, and the name of the settlement was changed to Scotia, reflecting the Nova Scotian heritage of its founders. Over the years Scotia grew from a haphazard arrangement of shacks to a well-ordered community of nicely painted homes. The company once operated its own store, saloon, bank, hotel, theater, hospital, and all the other facilities needed by the town.

16 For a popular article on Scotia, see Frank J. Taylor, "Paradise with a Waiting List," *Saturday Evening Post* (February 24, 1951).

30

Main Street, McCloud, California. Nestled at the base of Mt. Shasta,
McCloud is in an ideal location for anyone who enjoys outdoor
activities. This lumber-mill town was built by the McCloud
River Lumber Company, which once owned the town,
mill, and forest.

Early-day Timber Operations. Company-owned towns were frequently
located in the heart of America's timber land. Illustrated above is
the method once employed for taking redwood trees to the mill.

Courtesy Pacific Lumber Company

Korbel, California, as It Appeared in 1949. Owned by the Northern Redwood Lumber Company, Korbel existed only to support the operations of Northern's large lumber mill. Shown here (*left*) are the main housing area, log pond, lumber mill, and company offices. Across the Mad River are located the drying yards and an additional housing area occupied primarily by company officials and foremen. The rectangular building at the right of the log pond is a bunkhouse for single men. The post office, company store, theater, and other buildings are shown along with the company offices in the lower left.

Courtesy Ed C. Morrison

Lavender Pit, Near Bisbee, Arizona. This huge open-pit copper mine, opened in the 1950's, helps provide employment for residents of Bisbee. Most copper mining in the West now depends on the low-grade ore taken from such mines.

Entrance to Litchfield Park, Arizona. Operated by Goodyear Farms, a
subsidiary of Goodyear Tire and Rubber Company, Litchfield
Park is one of the most ornate company towns in the West.
It was the success of Goodyear's cotton experiment here
during World War I that made cotton an important
part of Arizona's economy.

Hayden, Arizona. The giant smelter of the Kennecott Copper Corporation completely dominates this company town. The town recently
has been sold for Kennecott by John W. Galbreath and
Company.

Company Housing, McCloud, California. Notice the board sidewalks—company towns were rarely provided with sidewalks of any kind.

Ajo, Arizona. The large copper refining plant and the huge open-pit
copper mine are the enterprises which give life to the town of Ajo.
Seen above is the older section of Ajo, nestled between the
plant and mine. The homes near the pit will gradually be
eliminated as the mine continues to expand.

Courtesy Phelps Dodge Corporation

Residents in Scotia take a great deal of pride in their community, and rightly so. The 304 houses in the town are always full, and there is a waiting list of people eager to move in. A three-bedroom home, with garage, electricity, and water furnished and garbage collected, rents for sixty dollars a month. The town is well maintained, and the tenants take great interest in keeping up their lawns and gardens. The company policy of awarding prizes each year contributes to this. The Pacific Lumber Company uses modern methods of forest management in its vast timber holdings, and Scotia will probably thrive for many years to come.

Scotia, however, has been affected by the changing economic pattern of the modern age. It is no longer an isolated community, since U.S. Highway 101 runs past the town. Other communities are within driving distance, and the company no longer finds it necessary to provide all the facilities it once did. The town's theater has been closed, the hospital has been eliminated, and all company-operated retail businesses have been turned over to private proprietors.

The company has strived to make Scotia a tourist attraction, incidentally perhaps advertising Pacific Lumber Company. In the center of town a small museum is maintained which tells the story of Scotia and of redwood lumbering in general. In addition, any tourist may take a self-guided tour through the giant mill at Scotia. Catwalks have been constructed above the mill operations and explanatory signs placed at strategic places so that the tourist may watch what happens to a giant redwood log from the time it enters the powerful "barker" until it becomes finished lumber.

In summary, the company town has played an important role in the development of the West's lumber industry. In early years many companies found it necessary to provide housing and community services for their employees as they established sawmills and logging headquarters in isolated areas. Company towns were often short lived as timber lands were cut away and mills moved on to other locations. With the building of modern highways, and as other advancements occurred in transportation, the need for company towns gradually has been eliminated. Mill sites may now be located farther away from logging operations and closer to population centers, while formerly isolated areas are now close enough to a town to allow employees to commute by automobile. Changing forest practices have eliminated some company towns and have contributed to the evolution of other towns into economically integrated, incorporated communities of home owners. A few companies, however, still find it to their advantage to operate towns in connection with their milling operations, and at least seventeen company-owned communities continue to exist today in the lumber regions of the West.

CHAPTER III

Copper Towns

THE COPPER INDUSTRY has been the basis for some of the West's largest and most permanent company towns. Phelps Dodge Corporation, for example, has owned the communities of Morenci and Ajo, Arizona, among the largest mining towns in the country, for nearly the entire century. Kennecott Copper Corporation once owned several communities in Arizona, Nevada, New Mexico, and Utah, and even though they are no longer company-owned, some of them remain as permanent and important communities of home owners.

The Mining Town

While not all towns connected with copper mines and smelters have been company-owned, in some cases the development of such towns was almost indispensable to the success of the companies. To illustrate, the director of public relations for Kennecott Copper's Chino Mines Division made some appropriate comments in 1961 on the development of the modern mining town:

> The complex machinery and the big smelters which began to grow toward the end of the last century meant jobs for others who went west and towns began to spring up and grow.
>
> So another dimension is added to the character of the miner: The need to work with other men—either to dig and process ore or to finance the big job of opening a mine. We may think romantically of the prospector as a man who is after solitude, and some may very well be that, but the man who develops a mine needs other people. To get their help, he has to know how to treat them.

33

Agricola [who published a scientific treatise on mining as early as 1556] again offers advice. He cautioned the mine operator to know many things—arithmetic, law, surveying and architecture. He also said he must know medicine ". . . that he may be able to look after his diggers and other workmen . . ." He also advised that mine owners look for a site (assuming there is a choice) where there are good roads and access to what we might call civilization. . . .

Whether necessity or tradition dictated it, then, the mining town was born. Quite often it was owned lock stock and barrel by the company which owned the mine for the simple reason that the company built the town. The houses were rented, usually for nominal prices, to the mine workers. A store was needed: The company built one and ran it, although the way was open for other merchants with a yen to "mine the miners." Hospitals, churches, schools, theaters and hotels—all were provided with the company footing the bill if necessary. Many of these facilities were the best available at the time. The hotels, in particular, some of which are still in operation, were rich and ornate. The towns grew up with an attitude of defiance as if to say to their relatives back east, "We're doing nicely, thank you, and we'll take care of our own as well as you can do."

Abuses and poverty? Corruption and dictatorship? Violence and intimidation? Certainly these were present, too. But the stories which I have heard indicate to me quite strongly that of the men who ran these towns, the overwhelming majority felt their sense of responsibility more keenly than their sense of power.[1]

A peculiar feature in the history of several copper company towns has been the reason for their longevity. Morenci, Ajo, Bisbee, and Ray, Arizona, all would have disappeared long ago if the nature of copper production had not changed. In the early years only high-grade ore, usually mined by tunnel, could be recovered profitably. But by the turn of the century Daniel C. Jackling, the young, imaginative president of Utah Copper Com-

[1] R. P. Saffold, Jr., speech delivered before Highlands University Workshop at Las Vegas, N.M., August 8, 1961.

pany, was pioneering in open-pit copper mining and in the recovery of 2 per cent ore. Because of his success the copper industry soon underwent a dramatic revolution, and the mining of ores carrying even less than 1 per cent copper became practical. Entire mountains, once thought worthless, were now converted into gigantic mines which breathed new life into some communities and led to the creation of others. In Arizona, almost 20 per cent of the copper produced comes from the large low-grade mines at Morenci, Ajo, Bisbee, Ray, Inspiration, Globe, Miami, Silver Bell, and San Manuel.[2]

Since low-grade mining tends to demand large-scale operations, a few copper communities have become company towns of unusual size. This is especially true when a smelter is located on the same property. At Ajo, for example, Phelps Dodge employs fourteen hundred and supports a town of about seven thousand population, while at Morenci two thousand people are employed supporting a community of about ten thousand.[3]

The Anaconda Company

Copper became Montana's chief metal product after the discovery in 1881 of the famed Anaconda lode by Marcus Daly. This was the bonanza which made Butte Hill known as the "richest hill on earth." An experimental smelter was soon constructed by William A. Clark, and in 1884 a large reduction works was completed at Anaconda, twenty-six miles west of Butte. In 1895 the Anaconda Copper Mining Company was organized, becoming the present Anaconda Company in 1956. Total mineral production of this company by 1956 exceeded five billion dollars in value.

Discovery of the Anaconda lode was responsible for the growth of Butte, Montana. While not a company-owned town, it was located on Daly's original claim, and its economy is still dominated

2 Frank J. Tuck, *Stories of Arizona Copper Mines* (Arizona Department of Mineral Resources, n.d.), 1.

3 Interview with H. E. Moore, office manager, Phelps Dodge Corp., Douglas, Ariz., March 12, 1962.

by the company. The company took little interest in the community or in the planning of it, however, until after 1946, when it began to back housing projects, invested in a hospital, and supported numerous recreational facilities.[4]

More like a company town was Anaconda, which was the pride and joy of Marcus Daly. This city was well planned from the beginning, but with the objective of making it a permanent community of home owners. Houses were built for sale to workers, merchants purchased lots in the predetermined business area, and the indomitable Daly spent one-half million dollars in an unsuccessful effort to make his town the capital of Montana.[5] Anaconda's town of Anaconda, therefore, developed in a more orderly fashion than the usual non-company town, but only with continual company interest and support.

Anaconda Copper, however, did develop a few full-fledged company towns in this century. Such a community was Conda, Idaho, which was built in 1921 to house employees at the company's phosphate mine. The town became a model village, consisting of several modern four-room cottages, a large residence for the superintendent, a boardinghouse for single men, an office building, a recreation hall, tennis courts, ball field, school, and a company store which was operated on a profit-sharing basis.[6] In 1959 the settlement was sold to the J. R. Simplot Company, which still owns it.

One of the most modern company-owned towns in the West is Anaconda's community of Weed Heights, Nevada, which supports the operation of the company's Yerrington mine and processing plant. The 87 per cent pure copper precipitate produced here is shipped by rail to the company's huge smelter at Anaconda.

The Weed Heights property was leased by the Anaconda Company in 1941. With the outbreak of hostilities in Korea in 1950,

4 "Company Town, 1956," *Time* (April 1, 1956), 100.
5 Isaac F. Marcosson, *Anaconda*, 54.
6 "Anaconda Copper Has Model Town at Conda, Idaho," *Engineering and Mining Journal*, Vol. CXXX, No. 5 (September 8, 1930), 240.

the federal government asked for increased copper production, and Anaconda decided to go all-out in developing the Yerrington mine. In 1951, A. E. Millar, the new general manager, arrived to begin opening the pit, constructing the metallurgical plant and building the town which would be necessary to bring employees to the middle of the Nevada desert. The company made a total expenditure of forty million dollars on these projects before a single pound of copper could be produced. Today, the 250 company-owned houses in Weed Heights are well maintained and rent for approximately thirty dollars a month, with water furnished free of charge and electricity and gas costing less than the amount paid by residents of nearby communities. About 70 per cent of the company's employees live in the company town.

At Weed Heights the company maintains a nine-hole golf course for its employees, as well as a swimming pool, bowling alley, and other recreational facilities. Following the trend in most modern company towns, Anaconda does not operate a store or other commercial facilities but permits private merchants to provide these services.

Anaconda's experience is significant in that it includes at least two broad phases of the story of company towns. First, community planning has been a necessary part of the development of the company itself because towns such as Anaconda, Conda, and Weed Heights were essential to the company's operations. Secondly, the various kinds of company-owned or company-dominated towns are represented: the company-built town of Anaconda, erected specifically to be sold; the full-fledged company town of Conda; and the highly attractive, modern company-owned community of Weed Heights, which still provides many community services but has eliminated nonessential operations such as the company store.

Kennecott Copper and Its Towns

Another of the West's large copper producers is Kennecott Copper Corporation, which once owned at least eight company

37

towns in Arizona, Nevada, New Mexico, and Utah. The development of Kennecott Copper is particularly significant here because one of its predecessors, Utah Copper Company, was responsible for developing the famed open-pit mine at Bingham. The success of this effort has helped account for the long existence of many company towns in the West. Kennecott is significant to the history of company towns also because its story includes the full cycle of company-town history: from the random mining community, to the planned smelter town, to the selling of entire communities to residents and private merchants.

Kennecott towns in Arizona were Ray and Hayden, both located about eighty miles southeast of Phoenix. Large-scale mining began at Ray in 1899 under an English company, but the property passed through several owners until Kennecott Copper Corporation acquired it in 1933. Open-pit mining operations began in 1950.

The several owners of Ray apparently worried little about planned community development, probably because the mine was frequently shutting down and the property was never considered a long-term operation. The business section of town, which was separated from the residential area, was leased to private merchants. The residential area was scattered in random fashion around the ever expanding pit. Various sections of town were built at different times and by mid-century gave the appearance of having been squeezed between the large piles of overburden which dominated the terrain and seemed to be inundating the town. After Kennecott sold its company towns to John W. Galbreath and Company in 1955, many residents at Ray purchased their own homes from this real-estate firm. It was generally understood that the entire town, or at least those homes that were purchased, would soon be moved to the Galbreath development at Kearny. The continued expansion of the pit made pre-emption of the townsite inevitable, and the town of Ray is now slowly dying.

The Mexican section of Ray, called Sonora, typifies a situation common to many company towns. The homes, nestled on a hillside a little farther from the mine, were erected by the Mexican workers themselves and were not as well built as other homes in town. They were built with little room between, in marked contrast to the rest of the homes in Ray which had as much space left between them as ordinary small-tract houses. The fact that a Mexican section existed, and that the Mexicans were allowed to build their own homes, is not uncommon among company towns in the Southwest.

While Ray simply grew in a rather desultory fashion, the town of Hayden was constructed in 1911 by the Ray Consolidated Copper Company as the center of its milling operations. The following year American Smelting and Refining Company built a smelter at Hayden. Ownership of most of the property, however, remained with Ray Consolidated until its merger with other companies, finally coming into the hands of Kennecott in 1933. In the 1950's Kennecott enlarged its operation and erected a new smelter. With the new construction two different companies had smelters in the town, but Hayden remained basically a Kennecott community.

When Hayden was first planned by Ray Consolidated it was publicized as the "model town of Arizona." The business and residential sections were well planned, and a Mexican settlement was provided for. This section still exists and appears to be typical of the poorly constructed, run-down "shanty town," although publicity of 1911 indicated that somehow the situation would be remedied.[7] The rest of the town was well laid out with an underground sewage system (something unusual in company towns of that day), street lighting, and graded thoroughfares. No company store existed, but merchants were allowed to lease property for private businesses, the only restriction being that but one saloon could operate in the community.

Ray Consolidated originally intended to sell homes to employees, but this plan did not materialize. It was only in 1954 that homes at last were sold to residents under Kennecott's new policy of getting

[7] *Arizona Daily Star*, August 13, 1911. (Article filed in clipping files of Pioneer Historical Society of Arizona, Tucson.)

out of the company-town business. Today Hayden stands as a thriving little incorporated community that is promised continued life because of the smelting operations which draw from the Ray mine as well as other sources.

Kennecott Copper Corporation was the owner of two Nevada towns, Ruth and McGill. Both began about 1908, belonging first to Nevada Consolidated Copper Corporation and later being taken over by Kennecott. When Kennecott retired from town ownership, housing at Ruth was in danger of becoming affected by the new underground operation of the "Deep Ruth" project, and was therefore sold for removal, as was the case at Ray. McGill, on the other hand, and the housing project known as New Ruth, were sold with the land.

Santa Rita, a mining town, and Hurley, where the smelter is located, were Kennecott's New Mexico company towns. Copper was discovered at Santa Rita in 1800 by the Spanish commandant in charge of military posts in the area. Santa Rita became a Spanish penal colony, and tradition holds that convict labor was used by its owners to develop the property.[8] Mining continued only sporadically for more than one hundred years until an American firm, the Chino Copper Company, began open-pit mining in 1909. The operation quickly became a success, and by 1913 some six thousand tons of ore a day were being processed at Santa Rita. The town which grew up included a company store, hospital, school, social hall, and theater.

The properties of the Chino Copper Company eventually became the Chino Mines Division of Kennecott Copper Corporation. Like so many other open-pit copper-mining towns, Santa Rita eventually was almost buried by its own excavations. The expansion of the mine led to the inevitable elimination of the town, and when company houses were sold the property did not go with them. The houses must be moved as the mine continues to eat away the hills of Santa Rita.

8 WPA Writers' Program, *New Mexico: A Guide to the Colorful State*, 264.

The smelter town for the Santa Rita mine is Hurley. Here a mill was built in 1910 by the Chino Copper Company, which later became the property of Kennecott. At the peak of its history as a company town Hurley consisted of 468 houses, a smelter, and several stores. In 1950 the population was over two thousand. It was sold along with the rest of Kennecott's towns, becoming an incorporated community in 1956.

When Kennecott Copper Corporation took over the Utah Copper Company, it inherited the famed open-pit mine at Bingham, Utah. Bingham was not a company town, but the community of Copperton was a company-owned settlement which had been built in the 1920's to provide for the overflow population from Bingham. Copperton was one of the most unique company towns in the West because of its use of copper to illustrate how this "everlasting metal" could be used in the building of homes. Such use of the company town as an advertising device was indeed unusual. House specifications called for such items as copper-clad strip shingles to be fastened with copper nails; copper valleys, hips, ridges, and downspouts were used, as well as copper gutter straps, downspout stays, and chimney saddles; and copper vents, bronze hardware and screens, and brass pipes, pipe fittings, and shower fixtures were specified.[9]

The smelter town of Garfield, Utah, was begun in 1906 and for a while supported both Utah Copper Company and American Smelting and Refining Company. Kennecott Copper succeeded to the ownership of the town, but when it disposed of the property all homes were either moved or abandoned. The smelter was closed, and the site of the former active community of Garfield remains today as nothing more than a ghost town.

Frequent reference has been made to the sale of Kennecott's company towns in 1955. Several important factors undoubtedly contributed to this move. Company towns had become an economic

[9] William Spencer, "Copperton—A Model Home Town for Utah Copper Employees," *Engineering and Mining Journal*, Vol. CXXV, No. 9 (March 3, 1928), 372.

burden that the company wanted to eliminate whenever possible. Some company officials felt continued paternalism was morally wrong, and further it was thought that company-town ownership did not make for the best labor relations.[10] A third factor may have been the multitudinous problems of community management which only detracted from the major goal of the company. Finally, it was felt that the need for the company town had disappeared as better transportation facilities made commuting to the mines and smelters no longer a problem. The elimination of Kennecott's company towns, therefore, in part reflects the rapid economic changes which have affected the entire West. As one newspaper editorial observed:

> The difference between the death of Garfield and most ghost towns of the Intermountain West is that instead of being the victim of a company's bankruptcy or the playing out of a natural resource, this town on the shores of Great Salt Lake is bowing out in recognition of the age of fast automobile transportation, the urbanization trend. Garfield's residents are resettling elsewhere in the wake of Kennecott Copper Company's decision to dispose of the property. The company town is as passé in most areas as the mule-drawn mine car.[11]

The sale of Kennecott's company towns was accomplished through John W. Galbreath and Company, of Columbus, Ohio. This real-estate firm had previously "sold" several company towns and continues to make this unusual function one of its specialties.[12] On December 15, 1955, the announcement was made, and the following day Galbreath representatives took over in each of the company's four divisions. Galbreath had purchased each town in its entirety and now began systematically to dispose of them. Newspaper accounts placed total assets at the Ray and Hayden town-

10 Interview with Charles D. Michaelson, general manager, Western Mining Division, Kennecott Copper Corp., Salt Lake City, Utah, August 6, 1961.

11 *The Salt Lake Tribune*, August 19, 1956.

12 For a cogent article on the activities of the Galbreath company, see Joseph P. Blank, "He Turned Company Towns into Home Towns," *American Business*, Vol. XXVIII, No. 9 (September, 1958).

42

sites at $600,000, while Hurley and Santa Rita together were valued at $1,500,000.[13]

In Arizona, the Galbreath company has erected a housing project of its own in the barren hills near Ray and Hayden. This well-planned village, named Kearny, consists of brick homes built mainly for sale to Kennecott employees as they decide to leave Hayden or Ray. The town has all modern facilities, including a small shopping center and an excellent motel, and it is far enough away from the smelter that fumes and smoke are no problem. No paternalism is felt here, for home owners are strictly on their own as far as maintenance and upkeep is concerned. Kearny is indeed an interesting development in an area so close to two old-time company towns.

Phelps Dodge Corporation

Phelps Dodge Corporation, along with Kennecott, is one of America's largest copper producers,[14] and this company, too, has been in part dependent upon the ownership of company towns. These towns, however, have had a history different from those of Kennecott in at least two respects. First, each of the two major communities, Ajo and Morenci, have both a mine and a smelter at the same location, which resulted in larger towns. Secondly, Phelps Dodge has no intention of eliminating its company towns, as Kennecott has done. The story of Phelps Dodge's involvement in company towns is an important example of the significance of these communities in Western mining.

Copper in the Clifton-Morenci area of Arizona was first discovered in 1864, and the Arizona Copper Company and the Detroit Copper Company became the two major producers in the area. By 1881 the Detroit Copper Company wanted to move its smelter from the Clifton area to Morenci but needed supplementary

---

13 *The Salt Lake Tribune*, December 15, 1955.
14 For a concise, readable history of Phelps Dodge, see Robert Glass Cleland, *A History of Phelps Dodge, 1834–1950*. Most of the following information about Morenci is based on this source and on Watt, "History of Morenci."

financing to do so. William Church, president of the firm, went to New York to find the necessary credit and soon contacted William E. Dodge, Jr., a partner in the Phelps Dodge Corporation. Church failed to obtain the loan, but he won Dodge's respect and aroused in him an interest in Arizona. Not long after this James Douglas, who eventually became a leader in Phelps Dodge's Western operations, had his first meeting with company officials. Upon learning that Douglas planned a trip to Arizona, Dodge commissioned him to examine Church's holdings at Morenci. This was a turning point in the history of Phelps Dodge, for Douglas' report was so favorable that the company agreed to purchase $30,000 worth of stock in the Detroit company.

By 1897 Phelps Dodge had assumed control of the Detroit Copper Company, together with a large share of the growing mining camp of Morenci. Already Morenci had some of the marks of a company town, with a company store, a hospital, and some company-owned dwellings. It was a typical rough-and-tumble mining camp with the business section composed largely of saloons, dance halls, and gambling houses. The residential section was largely a desultory collection of miner's "shanties." Fire soon destroyed the old town, and a new townsite was graded at the location of Morenci's present business section.

In 1901 a $61,000 company store, which still stands, was completed, as well as the elaborate Hotel Morenci. Also erected about the same time was the Morenci Club, which provided the town's residents with billiard and pool rooms, bowling alleys, baths, library, reading room, card room, gymnasium, and club rooms. The company was making definite efforts to improve life in the community beyond that of other old frontier mining camps.

By this time Morenci had become significant enough in Arizona's economy that the Gila Valley Bank decided to establish a branch there. Morenci's being a company town influenced the decision. Charles E. Mills, superintendent of the Detroit Copper Mining Company (then a subsidiary of Phelps Dodge), immediately invested $10,000 for one hundred shares of stock, making him the largest single stockholder in the expanded bank. Other company officials also subscribed. The bank was housed in the new hotel, occupying the same office as the Morenci Water Company and the Morenci Improvement Company, both owned by the mining company. M. E. Thorpe, secretary of the foregoing companies, was chosen to run the bank. This convenient arrangement was indeed an economic boon to the bank for its quarters were rent free, it paid the manager nothing, and the only expense to the bank was the hiring of an accountant to keep the books of all three concerns.[15]

The efforts of Phelps Dodge to improve living and working conditions at Morenci were not without problems. Satisfying the workingmen in a town such as Morenci, which had grown from an unplanned mining camp, was more difficult than in a community such as Tyrone, New Mexico, which was built from "scratch" by Phelps Dodge Corporation as a mining town. As explained by the author of a 1918 article on Tyrone:

> At the Morenci branch, the process of community improvement started much later in the life of the mine, and was carried on spasmodically, dependent upon the attitude and willingness of different managers. For this reason, although many things have been accomplished, the effect on the labor situation has been slight. There are instances of men who have been in the camp for 20 years or more who still harbor resentment owing to the fact that some perhaps very minor things that were wanted have not yet been secured and others took years to get. Less has actually been done in Tyrone than in Morenci, but in the latter place it is neither seen nor appreciated. This is due partly to the fact that much of the work was done many years ago, before the question of community development had assumed its present importance. Tradition, and without good reason, hurts Morenci as a place to live and work in, although the company is doing everything in its

[15] Ernest J. Hopkins, *Financing the Frontier: A Fifty Year History of the Valley National Bank*, 48–61.

power to better conditions by means of a constant program of development.[16]

In 1921 Phelps Dodge took over Arizona Copper Company's holdings, which gave it virtually complete control of Morenci and the surrounding area. Intensive development took place over the next decade, and in the 1930's it became necessary to provide additional housing. Many new homes were constructed at Morenci itself, and an entirely new area, called Stargo, was developed for additional housing. Recreational and school facilities were also expanded, and the company erected a $100,000 hospital. Increased production during and after World War II brought more workers to Morenci, which made it necessary for the company to provide still more housing. Another new area, called Plantsite, was developed. At both Stargo and Plantsite a branch of the company store was established. By the close of World War II it was estimated that Phelps Dodge had spent about $42,000,000 on the entire Morenci undertaking, which included plant expansion and housing development. The federal Defense Plant Corporation, which participated in many housing expansion projects during the war, had supplemented the Phelps Dodge investment with an additional $26,000,000. Today, Morenci is one of the largest and most active company-owned towns in the West, and has come a long way from the rollicking mining camp of the 1890's.

At the time Phelps Dodge became interested in the Morenci property it was also becoming involved with rich copper deposits near Bisbee. Here the fabulous Copper Queen mine was already producing rich ore, and when Phelps Dodge received an option to buy some adjacent properties, it did so with little hesitation. In 1885 the company acquired most of the stock of the Copper Queen, and a large-scale operation was begun under the name of the Copper Queen Consolidated Mining Company. For the next two

16 Charles F. Willis, "The Life of a Mining Community," *Engineering and Mining Journal*, Vol. CVI (October 26, 1918), 733.

decades Phelps Dodge was the only important mining company in this district, and the town of Bisbee was virtually dependent upon its operations.

Bisbee, like many other mining camps, did not develop as a consciously planned company town, although Phelps Dodge later acquired all the property upon which the community was built. Private saloons, stores, lumberyards, and other businesses found their way into town. The layout of the town could hardly be well planned, for its location in a narrow canyon compelled those who built houses to locate them wherever convenience dictated.

The company, however, tried to make life in Bisbee somewhat more pleasant than in the early days of gunfighting and lawlessness which once typified the camp. Local Y.W.C.A. and Y.M.C.A. chapters, largely supported by the company's directors, were organized around 1906. A new school and hospital were built, and a company-owned library was established. Not far from Bisbee, where the terrain allowed better community planning, the town of Warren was begun in 1906. As in Bisbee, the land belonged to the company, but the homes were to be privately owned.

The most infamous event in the history of Bisbee took place in 1917 when over 1,250 men were rounded up by the local sheriff's posse and deported in boxcars to Hermanas, New Mexico, with a warning never to return to Bisbee. This wartime labor disturbance was brought on by the I.W.W., which was attempting to organize the workingmen of the copper camps. The "Bisbee deportation" received widespread publicity and still remains in the memory of many as the most notable event in the colorful history of the town.[17]

Bisbee never became a fully-owned community in the sense that all homes and business houses were company property, but in recent years the company has found it necessary to provide more company-owned homes. In 1954 a new low-grade mine, the Lavender Pit, was opened, which brought a new influx of workers.

---

17 For an account of the Bisbee deportation, see Cleland, *History of Phelps Dodge*, 165–92.

The company built 140 homes, and this was the first time in Bisbee's history that any large number of company houses had existed.[18]

Two additional copper towns have been part of the Phelps Dodge empire: Ajo and Clarkdale, Arizona. At Ajo, mining began as early as 1854, and a typical mining camp grew up. About the turn of the century the New Cornelia Copper Company was formed, and the present town of Ajo gradually came into being. With the proved success of open-pit mining, the low-grade ore at Ajo became profitable, and the community prospered. It became a thriving, attractive desert community, and in 1931 the entire operation was purchased by Phelps Dodge.

The smelter for copper ore taken from the well-known mine at Jerome was located in the company-owned town of Clarkdale. Clarkdale was the pride of W. A. Clark, senator from Montana, who was one of the owners of the United Verde Copper Company. Founded in 1911, the town was well designed, and within five years it had achieved wide publicity as a model community.[19] About 1935 the United Verde stock passed into the hands of Phelps Dodge. Clarkdale remained a company town until about 1935, when the ore at Jerome gave out and the smelter was forced to close. The town was later purchased by a large cement company, which sold the homes but continued to operate a cement plant there.

Phelps Dodge, as we have observed, developed an attitude different from that of Kennecott in the matter of selling its company towns, and the reason for this is difficult to explain. The obvious difference between their economies is that at Morenci and Ajo both a smelter and a mine are in operation, and much of the land upon which the towns are located is marked for future mining. This prohibits the company from selling much of its property. Also Phelps Dodge seems to have become more involved with paternalistic enterprises such as company stores, recreational facilities, extensive hospital services, etc., and this involvement may have

18 H. E. Moore interview.
19 "Spotless Town," *Arizona*, Vol. VI, No. 6 (April, 1916).

developed a philosophy which is difficult to change. Again, the fact that Ajo and Morenci are much larger than any Kennecott town could present more problems than Kennecott experienced if the towns should be put up for sale. Whatever the reason, both corporations claim that their particular policy toward company towns brings employee satisfaction, and it is interesting that visits with employees of both companies reveal no great disparity in attitude toward management or in general contentment.

Since differences would be only in degree, it would be profitless here to discuss other copper towns. It is evident that copper-mining towns have played a significant part in the economic development of the West and that they have been important to the development of many copper-producing companies. These companies, in turn, have played a vital role in the economy of the West. In Arizona, the mining industry pays an average of $16,000,000 annually in taxes, carrying about 22 per cent of the total state tax load. In some localities, such as Morenci and Ajo, the company pays well over half the county taxes and is thus the chief supporter of schools and other local projects. The company town is significant, therefore, in much the same degree that the copper it produces is significant to the county, state, or nation.

CHAPTER IV

Coal-Mining Towns

Coal companies have received more unfavorable publicity in connection with their company towns than any other industry. The 1914 massacre at Ludlow, Colorado, deplorable sanitary conditions found in coal camps by federal commissions in 1923 and 1947, publicity given by unions to management's refusal to negotiate on housing and other social problems, and the fact that most coal camps, at least in the West, were located in areas which were at best difficult to make attractive have all contributed to the poor public image of company-owned towns in the coal fields.

The company town was essential in the development of the coal industry. In the early years of Western coal mining it was difficult to obtain workers unless the company provided living quarters for them. There was little incentive for home ownership near the mines, for there was little assurance that the mines would not someday close. Many miners came from foreign countries, especially from southern Europe, arriving in the coal fields practically penniless. The company town offered credit in the company store and a place to live. These considerations, together with the fact that mining companies needed to maintain ownership of property surrounding the mines for possible future development, all help explain the development of company-owned towns in the Western coal fields. The manager of the Albuquerque and Cerrillos Coal Company, of Madrid, New Mexico, put the issue this way:

It would have been difficult to operate the property other than as a company town. Miners were more or less of an itinerant group and generally without much finances. Many men came to work thru the instigation of friends and came direct from Italy, Czechoslovakia, etc. to Madrid and in most instances with practically no funds whatever. If the mines were to work this was about the only class of help that was available, so somebody had to provide a place for them to live and finance them until such time as they produced coal. . . . If anyone would have suggested at this time that a miner purchase his own home the miner would have thought it ridiculous, and the company, of course, wanted to maintain the town as a unit which they controlled.[1]

Living conditions in coal towns varied widely. Early camps established by Colorado Fuel and Iron Corporation and its predecessors were notably dirty and unsightly, with poor sanitary conditions, few opportunities for constructive social activity, and oppressive company control. At the other end of the scale was Phelps Dodge's coal town of Dawson, New Mexico, where good homes, fine community services, and a healthy community spirit prevailed. Most towns which developed after the 1920's were more responsibly planned and managed, and such communities as Gamerco, New Mexico, Hiawatha, Utah, and Mount Harris, Colorado, became noted as model mining towns. Older towns, too, improved as the century progressed. To generalize, although many coal towns represented the worst conditions among all company towns, others became desirable communities in every respect.

Western Coal Mining

Coal has been important to the economies of the states of Colorado, New Mexico, Utah, and Wyoming, and in each of these states a significant number of coal company towns have come and gone. In the first quarter of this century coal held first place in Colorado's mineral production, and between 1905 and 1930 this state produced an average of ten million tons annually. In its

---

[1] Letter from Oscar Huber, general manager, Albuquerque and Cerrillos Coal Co., Albuquerque, N.M., June 17, 1962.

developmental stage Colorado's coal industry was especially troubled with labor difficulties, some of which were the direct results of the squalid conditions in company towns. The most extensive deposit of coking coal in the West is found in the Colorado-New Mexico border area, and it is here that a large number of company towns have been located.

Almost the entire southwestern quarter of Wyoming is covered with a huge coal field known as the Green River Region. Mining began in this area as early as the 1860's when Union Pacific needed coal to "keep the black smoke belching into the sky."[2] In 1944 coal mining in Wyoming reached a peak of 9,846,000 tons annually, but by 1957 production had dropped to 2,117,000 tons, and since the 1940's Wyoming's coal company towns have disappeared. South of the huge Wyoming field lies the Uinta coal region, with major deposits in Carbon and Emery counties, Utah. The economy of these counties, especially Carbon County, has been largely dependent upon coal mining, and numerous company-owned towns have contributed to the maintenance of this field.

Much of the coal produced in the West has come from consumer-owned mines. The owning of their own mines was necessary for some companies whose primary operations demanded an assured source of fuel. At one time every transcontinental railroad system mined practically all its own coal.[3] Large metal mining companies did the same. Dawson, New Mexico, for example, furnished coal for the copper smelters of Phelps Dodge Corporation. Thus many company towns in the West were built to support companies whose primary interests were in enterprises other than coal, but to whom a continued supply of coal was essential. In Utah, for example, the coal-mining town of Columbia was owned, until 1946, by Columbia Steel Corporation. Sunnyside was originally owned by Utah Fuel Company, a subsidiary of the Denver and Rio Grande Western Railroad, and was purchased in 1951 by Kaiser Steel Corporation.

[2] *History of the Union Pacific Coal Mines, 1896 to 1940*, 28.
[3] A. T. Shurick, *The Coal Industry*, 263.

The Union Pacific Coal Company

When the Union Pacific Railroad began to span the continent, the necessity of maintaining a permanent supply of coal led to the opening of mines in Wyoming and to the establishment of a number of company-owned towns. The first mining town to be created by the company was Carbon, Wyoming, where settlement began as early as 1868. This rugged little community did not become a real company town, but it was a typical frontier coal-mining settlement and had some of the marks of a company town. It represents the first step in the development of company towns in Wyoming and therefore holds some significance here.[4]

Carbon was on railroad property, but privately owned residences sprang up rapidly. Many of them were nothing more than caves covered in front with boards and earth with stovepipes poking out of holes in the roofs. The railway company hauled water from Medicine Bow, dumping it into a wooden cistern which served the town. The community soon became quite active, with a business district consisting of several saloons, three general stores (including a company store), a shoe shop, a barbershop, and a blacksmith. Also established were churches, a dance hall, and a school. Reaching a peak population of approximately three thousand, after thirty-five years the town was closed, leaving the area desolate.

Cumberland, Wyoming, also built by Union Pacific, was more typical of the company town. It was opened around 1900 with tents and bunkhouses set up around the prospecting area. A town was eventually constructed, a commissary was opened, and coal mining was carried on until 1930. Hundreds of people were on hand for the closing celebration of that year. Other Union Pacific towns in Wyoming included Dana, Superior, Reliance, and Winton. In other areas, such as Rock Springs, the company carried on extensive coal mining but did not find it necessary to operate towns.

4 Information about Carbon taken from *History of the Union Pacific Coal Mines*, 28–36; and WPA Writers' Program, *Wyoming: A Guide to Its History, Highways, and People*, 350.

The community which best represents the development of company towns in Wyoming is Hanna. Hanna passed through almost every stage possible in the rise and decline of a company town, from a community of tents, through the fully developed paternalistic town, to its present status as a small, declining village of home owners. Its story began when ore at the Carbon mine declined and excellent new deposits were discovered near the present site of Hanna. Union Pacific opened two mines in 1889, and a camp was established with the usual primitive living conditions. Winter cold and heavy snow, together with the fact that Hanna was still simply a tent town, made life difficult that first season. Original settlers came largely from the Carbon mine, and when the latter closed in 1902, Hanna provided new employment for many of its miners.

Union Pacific was determined to build at Hanna a town which was something more than the typical frontier coal camp. Streets were laid out, and relatively comfortable homes were soon erected. These rented for twelve dollars a month, including water. The town was named for the wealthy industrialist and politician Marcus Hanna.

The company owned and controlled everything in Hanna, including the school. The town was operated with a kind of "enlightened" paternalism which developed an unusual attachment to the town, if not to the company, among many of its residents. Present townsmen are largely former company employees who have purchased their homes and retired. One such man said in 1961 that after living in Hanna for seventy years and giving fifty-three years of service to the company, he and his wife simply wanted to remain there the rest of their lives, even though they could have moved elsewhere.[5] Another long-time resident moved to Laramie but still declares with nostalgia that "someday Hanna will come back," if not as a mining town at least as the prominent community it once was.[6]

5 Interview with O. C. Buehler, Hanna, Wyo., July 6, 1961.
6 Interview with Henry Jones, Laramie, Wyo., July 8, 1961.

In order to support social activity in Hanna, the company provided a community recreation hall, where frequent dances were held, and allowed various fraternal societies to function. The company also built and leased to a private party for operation a lodge hall which included a movie house, pool hall, bar, candy kitchen, and lodge room. In addition, the company made monthly contributions to a community fund, which was also supported by rental received from private parties at the hall. This fund provided, among other things, an annual Christmas party at which every child in the community received candy, oranges, and a gift.

In addition to housing and recreational facilities, the company operated a store, hotel, and hospital. The store gave credit through the scrip system, but it does not appear that the company attempted to be oppressive or to force its employees to trade at the store. While it is true that many people found themselves perpetually in debt to the company store, it is also true that the company willingly carried them on the books during periods of depression and unemployment, though limiting their purchases to necessities.[7]

When attempts at union organization were made in the early years of the twentieth century, some companies took advantage of their positions as property owners and landlords in their attempts to frustrate union efforts. At Hanna, organizers were not allowed on company property, hence they could not enter the town, and detectives were hired to keep them out. The workers nevertheless were determined to organize, and when union men let it be known that they would be in a horse and buggy on a county road, off company property, the miners met them there and received union cards.[8] The union was finally established at Hanna, but it had little effect upon the actual operation of the town.

The first school building in Hanna was erected by the company and later turned over to the school district for $15,000. Although the local school board was elected, for many years it was practically

[7] *Ibid.*
[8] O. C. Buehler interview.

a foregone conclusion that at least one company representative would be a member, giving the company a strong voice in school policies. The company, of course, could control school funds, but that it was not malicious in this power may be seen in the problem which arose in the 1940's relative to the erection of a new high school building. Henry Jones, a company employee, was elected to the school board in 1940 and soon became president. Overcrowded conditions prevailed, but the company had long opposed construction of a new building. Officials argued that if the mines closed down in the near future, the expense would not have been justified. Jones, however, persistently continued to present his case to the company president, who finally agreed to the project. A new high school was built at a cost of $146,000, but within eight years the mines were closed and, noted Jones, "we were flatter than pancakes and didn't need all that room."

In 1936 Hanna became an incorporated community, which was unusual for company towns. Among other things, this gave the town government, still under *de facto* control of the company, the privilege of licensing saloons and other businesses in which the company did not want to become directly involved. It is reported that one reason for the incorporation was to bring saloons into Hanna so that men would not lose work time by going to the little town of Elmo to drink. Whatever the intent, the local government was formed, and elections were regularly held. As might be suspected, the company superintendent usually was elected mayor.

About 1950 the last coal mine at Hanna closed, but the town did not completely disappear. The company offered its houses for sale at approximately one hundred dollars a room, and under these terms many individuals purchased the homes they had been renting. The land remained in the hands of the company but was leased to home owners for one dollar a year. Hanna is no longer an active mining community, but it continues as a small, quiet town which gives the appearance of gradual decline. The company store, the community hall, the company offices, several unsold company houses, and the high school all stand vacant as silent reminders of the town's flourishing past. In the hearts of some, however, the past still lives, as old-timers such as Henry Jones remain determined that "Hanna will come back."

Southern Colorado

The most intense and perhaps most just criticism of company-owned towns in the West has centered around those established in the coal fields of southern Colorado. Here Colorado Fuel and Iron Corporation controlled more towns than any other company in the West. Charges and counter-charges confuse the true picture, but a review of these arguments is important to an understanding of the role played by the company town in the social unrest prevailing in the coal fields in the early years of the twentieth century.

Coal operations began in Colorado as early as 1864, and Colorado Fuel and Iron Corporation, a conglomerate of many smaller companies, became the largest producer before the end of the century. Some of its mines were located near established communities such as Walsenburg. In most cases, however, mines were located in areas not easily accessible by roads. Often they were in canyons, and the supporting communities were built on hillsides or in narrow ravines. As coal mining expanded, the activity of union organizers also increased. The United Mine Workers Union, established in the state in 1890, soon won recognition in the northern fields. In southern Colorado, however, where Colorado Fuel and Iron dominated, unionization was thwarted for many years.

Among other things, the management of company towns came under harsh union scrutiny. Owners were charged with maintaining complete economic and political control, denying freedom of speech, providing only the most wretched living conditions, and refusing to do anything to aid in the social betterment of company employees. Barron R. Beshoar, deeply sympathetic with the plight of the coal miners, gave the following report in 1943:

> The single men lived in company-owned boarding houses and

57

those with families in company-owned shanties, barren little homes that reared their weather-beaten boards above piles of ashes and tin cans. Public roads ran through the cañons, but at the approach to each camp a gate and a sign, "Private Property— Keep Out," barred the way. Armed guards, employed by the coal company and deputized by the sheriff of the county watched over the gates and kept order in the camps. The term "to keep order" had an interpretation all its own in the coal camps. Men could get as drunk as they pleased in the company saloon, carouse about with daughters of joy, and brawl with fists or knives without undue interference from the camp marshal or his deputies. It was only when strangers made their way into camps on business considered inimical to the company, or when the miners found fault with their way of life that the marshal's brand of order was rigidly enforced. Fault-finders, individual or collectively, were not tolerated in these closed camps. Intruders and malcontents were ferreted out by an intricate espionage system and treated by heavily-armed guards to the kangaroo, the coal district term for a professional beating. Along with the kangaroo went the dread sentence of "Down the cañon." And to go "down the cañon" meant blacklisting and starvation—or exile.[9]

Other charges were that coal operators maintained political control of their communities through strict regulation of voting, and that anyone voting against the interests of the company was in danger of losing his job. Polls frequently were located on company property, and it was charged that if employees did not sufficiently outnumber "outsiders," entrance to the closed camps would be denied the latter, or precinct boundaries could be drawn in such fashion as to exclude them.[10]

Evidence of this kind of political skulduggery is seen in a *Monthly Labor Review* report on the Huerfano County election

---

[9] Barron R. Beshoar, *Out of the Depths: The Story of John R. Lawson a Labor Leader*, 21.

[10] George P. West, *U.S. Commission on Industrial Relations Report on the Colorado Strike*, 57.

in 1914.[11] Incumbent Sheriff J. D. Farr, accused of being a puppet of the coal company, was ostensibly re-elected, but his opponent, as well as the opponents of other officials elected at the same time, contested the results. The state supreme court found that not long before the election new voting precincts had been created with boundaries practically identical with borders of the company towns. Permission of company officials was required before anyone could enter the premises. In other cases precincts were so gerrymandered as to make it necessary for qualified voters to go as far as eighteen or twenty miles to cast their ballots. It was found that union organizers, merchants, delivery men, and friends of the workers were excluded from company camps during the election and that the holding of political meetings was practically impossible.

Voluminous testimony was given before the court concerning coercion and intimidation, although the accuracy of much of the testimony is questionable. An important point, however, was that illiterate voters were furnished with cards enabling them to vote the way the company desired. The result, declared the court, was not really an expression of opinion or an intelligent exercise of suffrage, but plainly a coal-company dictated vote. The court ruled that the vote of the closed precincts should be thrown out and that the election should be decided by the results in other precincts of the county. As a result, Farr and other company-sponsored candidates were eliminated and their opponents installed in office.

Prior to the 1914 strike the union had made many other charges. John R. Lawson, chief organizer, held secret meetings off company property and slowly convinced workers that they needed to organize. Among the abuses cited by Lawson was the scrip system, which he said compelled miners to accept company scrip and to

11 " 'Industrial Necessity' for Political Control: An Incident in the Colorado Miner's Strike," *Monthly Labor Review*, Vol. III, No. 2 (August, 1916), 35–37.

buy only in company-owned stores at exorbitant prices. He decried the requirement that miners buy their blasting powder from the company at high prices. He also criticized coroner's juries which he accused of finding deaths actually caused by lack of proper company safety precautions as due to a miner's own negligence. Lawson charged also that the mails were watched, and that those who received letters, magazines, or newspapers from sources considered inimical to management were in danger of a trip "down the cañon."[12] It is little wonder that Colorado Fuel and Iron was eager to get him out of the area.

Antagonists also charged that the company denied the right of free speech by discharging employees who spoke too soon, and that even school teachers and ministers were shackled by company censoring. Although little evidence could be produced to prove that such people had been released solely because of their anti-company statements, a letter from J. F. Welborn, president of the company, to an attorney in New York suggested the power held by the company. With reference to Daniel McCorkle, minister in the company-owned town of Sunrise, Wyoming, Welborn wrote:

> At the time of the Ludlow affair the minister was very outspoken in his criticism of the coal companies, but seemed to regret his action when informed of the facts concerning that disturbance. He has socialistic tendencies, however, and I have been informed that his wife is a Greek, yet they may both be perfectly honest. . . . We have thought some of changing the minister at Sunrise, but have refrained from taking a course that would be unfair to him or would incite a prejudice against him because of what may have been simply indiscreet statements in connection with the Ludlow outbreak.[13]

It is evident that the company could, if it wished, dismiss the minister, and that management would have felt no moral repugnance at such a move. On the other hand, it is also evident that

12 Beshoar, *Out of the Depths*, 9–10.
13 West, *Report on the Colorado Strike*, 56.

Welborn was making every effort to be fair-minded about the situation.

Another complaint frequently heard concerned the intense racial animosities which existed in the Colorado coal fields. Company superintendents and company-controlled marshals were accused of actually encouraging such antagonism "on the theory that the more the men were divided the less likely they were to exchange ideas and discuss possible grievances."[14]

The Company's Viewpoint

From management's point of view, these charges were without foundation, or were made without an understanding of the problems facing them in the operation of mining properties. George Kindel, a congressman from Colorado, defended management in a Washington speech on June 13, 1914:

> The mine owner is neither a brute nor a fool; he will not knowingly subject his property to destruction nor his men to unnecessary danger. Selfish interest alone dictates a contrary policy. Aside from this, I may say that I am personally acquainted with many of the operators of my State, and I know them to be honorable and humane men, who entertain a keen solicitude for the welfare of their employees.[15]

During the 1913–14 labor difficulties, the operators replied to union criticism with a counter-attack upon the union itself. Several companies independent of Colorado Fuel and Iron wrote a letter to the President deploring union action and criticism. The sole purpose of the strike, they declared, was to force recognition of the United Mine Workers, which actually had a membership of only about 10 per cent of the men employed in the area. Furthermore, they complained, the union had deviated from this original

14 Beshoar, *Out of the Depths,* 1–2.

15 *The Struggle in Colorado for Industrial Freedom* (bulletin issued periodically by coal operators in Colorado during the 1914 labor difficulties), Bulletin No. 4 (July 6, 1914), 2.

purpose in making other needless demands, and the strike had become simply lawlessness and anarchy.[16]

In December, 1901, Colorado Fuel and Iron began publication of *Camp and Plant*, a company organ designed for employee consumption. Among other things, this periodical was obviously intended to improve the company image among employees themselves. *Camp and Plant* lasted only a few years, but it portrayed quite a different picture of company attitude than that presented by the union and other critics. The opening issue, for example, announced that the publication would promote the work of the Sociological Department, which had helped establish night schools, kindergartens, libraries, cooking schools, clubs, and musical groups at the many company camps.[17] Succeeding issues described in great detail these and other projects conducted by the company for the social betterment of its employees. Among other things, a cooking teacher was employed to travel from camp to camp giving instruction to women and even to interested men. Lectures on a wide variety of subjects were also sponsored, as were social gatherings a number of clubs. Kindergartens established by the company were used to help overcome differences in nationalities, on the assumption that it was easier to teach new language and customs to children than to adults.

Camp and Plant also revealed efforts of the company constantly to improve housing and sanitary conditions in the various camps. Improvement of old homes, cleaning of wells and cisterns, and other community improvement projects were frequently described in an obvious effort to combat the barrage of criticism which coal camps had begun to receive.

Company relationships to the public schools were also discussed. Readers were told that it was company policy not to interfere with the schools but to aid them. The company declared its interest in

16 *Ibid.*, Bulletin No. 1 (June 22, 1914), 3.
17 *Camp and Plant*, Vol. I (December 14, 1901), 1.

Stargo Housing Area at Morenci. This new housing area demonstrates how terrain determines the layout of company towns. Here the company has terraced the hillsides in order to provide housing areas.

Company Foreman's Home, Hayden, Arizona. This house, though less pretentious than the general superintendent's home, was somewhat more comfortable than houses provided for common laborers. The house was purchased by its occupant when the town was sold.

General Superintendent's Home, Hayden, Arizona. This is the largest home in Hayden.

Company Store at Hanna, Wyoming. The old store building stands idle today as a silent reminder of the days when this company town flourished.

Recreation Hall, Frontier, Wyoming. This hall, idle for many years, is typical of the recreation halls provided in many early coal-mining communities.

Morenci, Arizona. Morenci, still completely owned by Phelps Dodge
Corporation, sprawls over the hills. Here is shown the downtown
area, including the theater, shopping center, and teachers'
dorms located behind the shopping area. On the right is
the Phelps Dodge office building.

Phelps Dodge Company Store, Morenci, Arizona. Phelps Dodge Mercantile Company still operates several company stores in Arizona. Outside the Phelps Dodge organization very few company stores still exist in the West. "P. D. Merc.," as it is dubbed by employees, is a profit-making organization, although its prices are competitive with other stores. Behind the store can be seen part of the company-owned Hotel Morenci. Above the store is the company hospital.

The Old Company Store at Helvetia, Arizona. Never a full-fledged company town, Helvetia was an early settlement consisting mostly of privately owned tents and huts. The old store has long since disappeared.

Courtesy Pioneer Historical Society of Arizona

good education and pointed out that it had even established night schools for young men who worked in the mines during the day.

In spite of these disclaimers, company dictation in the matter of selecting teachers did exist. The Reverend Eugene S. Gaddis, superintendent of the Sociological Department until February, 1915, later testified that company officials dictated the selection of teachers and obtained the dismissal of those to whom they objected, even though it meant appointing incompetent teachers.[18] The extent of such arbitrary action, however, is not clear.

In reply to the allegation that the company used camp marshals to browbeat residents into submission to arbitrary policies, Colorado Fuel and Iron again presented a contrasting story. Camp marshals, said a company spokesman, were often regularly elected constables and were employed only in the larger camps:

> Their general duties are very much the same as those of the peace officer in villages and small towns throughout the United States. In addition, they have charge of the sanitary conditions of the camps and the general repair and care of tenant houses. . . .
>
> The camp marshals are neither "gunmen" nor thugs, and are chosen for the duties assigned to them with the same view to their fitness for that work that is exercised in the selection of other employes for particular work.
>
> The marshal is often the one man in the camp to whom the employes tell their troubles, both real and imaginary.
>
> He does not, as is charged, assault the miners, and they are free to complain of him or anyone else without danger of being discharged.[19]

Here, however, management did not effectively answer the charge that elected marshals were dictated to by the company, and that rather stringent methods were used to combat possible union activities. Furthermore, while the company was probably correct

18 West, *Report on the Colorado Strike*, 56.

19 *The Struggle in Colorado for Industrial Freedom*, Bulletin No. 15 (September 4, 1914), 1–2.

in saying marshals were employed only in the larger camps, implying such officers were few in number, it ignored the critics' concern with the deputies which were appointed from time to time. Company defense of its security policies left something to be desired.

Defending the scrip system, which was said to keep real money away from employees and prohibit them from purchasing goods anywhere but at the company store, J. F. Welborn stated that during the fiscal year preceding the 1914 strike employees received 80.9 per cent of their earnings in cash. During the same year miners worked an average of 248.5 days at $4.02 a day and received an average of $800.00 in cash.[20]

The truth about company towns in southern Colorado probably lies somewhere between the opposite views just discussed. Although living conditions left much to be desired, the company did take some interest in community betterment, and certain economic and social problems may well have delayed more rapid progress. The scrip system was perhaps not as oppressive as its critics charged. Abuses undoubtedly existed in the matter of political control, but in this age of fierce competition one might almost expect such a company to use every possible tool in squelching criticism of the economic policies which seemed to maintain it.

An Eruption and Its Aftermath

Coal companies naturally resisted all efforts at union organization, and the company town became a useful tool in this battle. Candidly replying to a query about the difficulties involved in organizing miners living in company-owned towns, one union official declared:

> These company-owned towns were barricaded, either by wood or wire with a guard at every entrance and egress and unless the miner and his family were identified they had no entrance nor egress to the operation. Persons not connected with the company . . . were not permitted in these company towns without per-

[20] West, *Report on the Colorado Strike.*

64

mission of the superintendent of the camp. This, of course, made it especially difficult in trying to organize miners, who lived in company-owned towns, since union organizers were prohibited from entering any company camp and the only contacts with the miners would be when the miners were permitted off the property, usually on a Sunday when they went to the towns nearest the coal camps and this was not very often.[21]

In September, 1913, the smoldering discontent of the miners finally burst out in a general strike in southern Colorado. Strikers were quickly ordered from their homes in company-owned towns, and thousands packed up their few belongings and filed into tent colonies established by the union. The state militia was called in to keep order, but violence erupted. The union charged Colorado Fuel and Iron with hiring strikebreakers and inciting violence, while the company lodged countercharges against the union. Several armed skirmishes took place, but the high point in the struggle came in April, 1914, at the union's tent colony of Ludlow. Here an armed clash occurring between the militia and the miners resulted in a tent's catching fire and burning to death two women and eleven children who had taken refuge in a pit under the wooden floor. At least twenty-one people were killed that day. Enraged strikers took control of almost the entire southern coal field, and fighting did not cease until June, when federal troops arrived on the scene. The "Ludlow massacre" was widely publicized throughout the nation, with union and management again making charges and countercharges.[22]

One result of this tragic strike was the establishment of an employees' representation plan which was widely copied by other companies in the nation until it was outlawed in 1938 as a

[21] Letter from Fred K. Hefferly, secretary-treasurer, United Mine Workers of America, Denver, Colo., April 18, 1962.

[22] For the union side of the argument, see *United Mine Workers Journal*, Vol. LX (April 1, 1949), in which it is claimed that the attack on Ludlow was an "unprovoked assault" of strikebreakers and company thugs. For management's side, see *The Struggle in Colorado for Industrial Freedom*, Bulletin No. 8 (July 25, 1914), in which it is declared that strikers precipitated the battle.

"company union." The "Industrial Representation Plan and Agreement" did not completely soothe the troubled waters, however, as the union maintained steady progress in its efforts to organize. By 1933 practically all the miners in the United States had joined John L. Lewis' United Mine Workers of America. Since then union leaders have helped change company-town conditions by eliminating the scrip system and its alleged abuses and negotiating on other items such as house rent.

Under its new plan, meanwhile, the company made significant strides in the direction of improving its towns, and in 1917 it reported on the first two years of progress. According to the report 164 new houses had been built and 250 were under construction. Every lot had been fenced, and each house was to be screened before the end of the summer. Improvement of water and drainage systems at several camps was reported, and a "sanitary toilet" had been adopted for use in all camps. New dispensaries had been erected or were planned at several camps, five new school buildings or additions had been erected, and company-sponsored training in the manual arts, domestic science, and first aid had been extended. The company had turned its clubhouses over to the Y.M.C.A., which was operating sixteen branch associations. Religious activity was being encouraged, as well as all kinds of sports and social activity, and the company was contributing financially to such groups as the Boy Scouts and the Camp Fire Girls.[23]

If later issues of company periodicals are accurate, Colorado Fuel and Iron continued to make significant and commendable strides in improving all aspects of community life. Shade trees were planted in all the camps. The company began to encourage regular community meetings which, in 1927, were reported to be a popular success. It also made efforts to "Americanize" its foreign workers through classes in English, classes in American ideals and government, and organization of "America First Societies."

23 *Colorado Fuel and Iron Industrial Bulletin,* Vol. II (July 31, 1917), 3–6.

Under its new representation plan, the company even began to bargain with employees concerning housing rates. A 1915 agreement set rent at two dollars a room. Two years later, however, the company asked for new negotiations. Since 1915 houses had been fenced, systematic clean-up of the camp had been established, and coal and chicken houses had been provided. The company declared that these things had already cost over $98,000. Considering such expenditures, plus taxes, depreciation, and the company's feeling that it was entitled to a 5 per cent annual return on its investment, the company called for rent to be increased to three dollars a room. A series of joint conferences were held, and a compromise settlement of $2.50 a room was agreed to. The mere fact that such negotiations could occur illustrates the gradual change taking place in the atmosphere of the company town.[24]

Despite these improvements life in many coal towns still left much to be desired. In 1923 a federal commission investigated the entire coal industry, and its voluminous report[25] revealed that shabby housing, unsanitary community facilities, and other abuses still existed throughout the nation. Twenty-four years later a medical survey was made of the bituminous coal industry by the Coal Mines Administration. A variety of conditions was reported, but it was evident that poor conditions still existed in many camps, including those of the West, although no specific company or town was mentioned.[26] By that time, however, company-owned towns in the West were on the wane, and by the 1960's they had practically disappeared.

In the early part of this century a new trend developed in connection with new company towns coming into existence. A number of companies began to build model coal-mining communities, and

24 *Ibid.*, Vol. XI (June, 1927), 13–14; and (October, 1927), 14.

25 U.S. Coal Commission (John Hays Hammond, chairman), *Report of the United States Coal Commission, Dec. 10, 1923.*

26 U.S. Coal Mines Administration, *A Medical Survey of the Bituminous Coal Industry. Report of the Coal Mines Administration.*

these improved greatly upon conditions thought typical of the company town. Such a community was Gamerco, New Mexico.[27] The Gallup American Coal Company, which owned the town, was in turn owned by three large copper companies for whose plants it supplied coal. The town, founded in 1921, was a consolidation of three old, typical coal camps then existing in the company fields. The engineering firm hired to do the developing made of Gamerco a well-planned, model community which continued as a company town until 1945.

Disappearance of the Coal Town

As with other kinds of company towns, vast economic changes in America have largely accounted for the disappearance of company-owned coal towns. Differing interpretations have been placed on the significance of this move. One coal company manager, for example, felt that the company town was a benefit to the worker but that union haggling over rates, prices, housing rentals, etc., had led to the elimination of them.[28] A Colorado union official, on the other hand, felt that company towns were detrimental to the welfare of workers, and he took pride in attributing their elimination partly to union influence.[29]

It seems evident, however, that one must look farther than the mere existence of the union to account for the disappearance of coal company towns, and that two basic economic changes are more directly responsible. First, the coal business itself has declined in recent years, largely owing to changes in fuel demands. Oil and natural gas have widely replaced coal as the fuel for industrial as well as home use, although steel companies still demand good coking coal. Railroads have switched to diesel fuel. The decline in demand for coal has led naturally to a decline in the number of

[27] The story of the building of Gamerco may be found in H. B. Cooley, *Story of a Complete Modern Coal Mine*, reprint in booklet form of a series of articles in *Coal Age* (August-September, 1923).

[28] Interview with V. O. Murray, president and general manager, Union Pacific Coal Co., Rock Springs, Wyo., July 6, 1961.

[29] Fred K. Hefferly letter.

men employed and to the closing of many small, more isolated operations. In Colorado, for example, the number of men employed in coal mining declined from a peak of 13,117 in 1923 to 3,238 in 1953.[30] With the closing of the coal mines, the company towns naturally disappeared.

A second economic change which has helped eliminate the coal company town is, of course, the improvement in transportation facilities which has also affected the towns of other industries. The publicity director of Colorado Fuel and Iron Corporation in 1962 indicated his belief that this is the most overriding reason why company towns have almost disappeared.[31] Few mines are so isolated today that workers cannot commute from nearby non-company settlements. With few exceptions, therefore, the company-owned coal town in the West has become a thing of the past.

30 Hubert E. Risser, *The Economics of the Coal Industry*, 106.
31 Letter from Algird C. Pocius, director of publicity, Colorado Fuel and Iron Corp., Pueblo, Colo., September 11, 1962.

ALTHOUGH COMPANY TOWNS in the West have been most significant in the production of coal, copper, and lumber, other
businesses have also created a few such communities. These towns
are of only minor importance to the industries involved, but their
total number justifies brief mention of at least a few. Their isolated
location, their dependence upon a single enterprise, and the fact
that their existence was usually essential to company success in
their respective locations gave them much in common with other
company-owned villages.

Miscellaneous Towns

The hectic gold rushes of the nineteenth century produced no
company towns, but it is interesting to observe that a few company-
owned communities have been connected with gold mining in this
century. Hammonton, California, founded in 1905, and Stibnite,
Idaho, both now abandoned, are two examples. Iron mining, too,
has produced a few company towns, such as Eagle Mountain,
California, a modern community owned by Kaiser Steel Corporation. Begun in 1947, the isolated Eagle Mountain mine provides
ore for Kaiser's huge steel plant at Fontana, California.

Oil companies have also created a few towns in connection with
certain isolated refineries, and Sinclair, Wyoming, is an outstanding example. Founded in the 1920's, it was originally named
Parco. In 1934, along with the refinery, it was purchased by Sinclair. During the first half of this century Midwest Refining Company owned Midwest, one of the largest company towns in

Wyoming. The modern trend in company-built towns is represented by Richfield Oil Corporation's refinery town of New Cuyama, California. The town was founded in 1950, but homes were sold to employees in a typical modern effort to avoid the problems of paternalism.

Certain kinds of manufacturing plants are ideally located some distance from population centers and have sometimes given rise to company towns. The cement manufacturing town of Boettcher, Colorado, for example, was founded in 1926 and is still owned by Ideal Cement Company. Davenport, California, was built in 1906–1907 to house workers of the Santa Cruz Portland Cement Company, although it was actually owned by a land company on whose property the plant was located. Manufacturers of high explosives have also found it necessary to locate away from large population centers and sometimes to create towns of their own. Louviers, Colorado, and DuPont, Washington, were part of a chain of model company towns once owned by E. I. Du Pont de Nemours and Company. As explained by a company official:

> The company town was an economic necessity during the early part of the 20th Century when the nature of an operation dictated that it be isolated from population areas. The employees were unable to travel farther than a few miles from home to place of work, unless special train service could be arranged and was justified. Explosive plants required isolation and therefore, a company village for all employees was an absolute necessity.[1]

Unique in its history is Litchfield Park, which was built by the men who launched the cotton industry of Arizona.[2] In 1916 Goodyear Tire and Rubber Company faced a problem. It had developed a new cord tire which promised Goodyear undisputed leadership

[1] Letter from E. E. Stewart, special assistant to production manager, E. I. Du Pont de Nemours & Co., Wilmington, Del., June 6, 1962.

[2] The story of Litchfield Park may be found in Hugh Allen, *The House of Goodyear: A Story of Rubber and of Modern Business*; and Susan M. Smith, "Litchfield Park and Vicinity" (unpublished Master's thesis, Department of History, University of Arizona, 1948).

71

in the industry, but its success hinged upon an ample supply of the tough, flexible, long-staple cotton which could be obtained only from Egypt or from the coastal areas of Georgia, Florida, and the Carolinas. The supply of Egyptian cotton was seriously threatened by the international crisis, and the villainous boll weevil had begun to raise havoc with American producers, causing domestic prices to soar. Hope was seen, however, in Department of Agriculture experiments conducted in Arizona which had demonstrated that the extra-strength, long-staple cotton, so essential to the new tire, could be produced in this arid state. So it was that in 1916 the Southwest Cotton Company was formed, a subsidiary of Goodyear, and some twenty-six thousand acres of land were leased not far from the city of Phoenix. A work force was organized which consisted of two thousand men, one thousand mules, and a fleet of caterpillar tractors, and by the end of the following year four thousand acres were under cultivation and several thousand bales of cotton had been shipped to the Goodyear factory. The success of this huge enterprise was largely responsible for making cotton one of the major industries in this state of cactus, cattle, and copper.

The Goodyear company had outlined for itself a formidable task which included not only technical problems but also human problems. Imported laborers, builders, mechanics, and supervisors all had to be housed and cared for, and Goodyear suddenly found itself in the curious process of community planning and town building. Small villages and camps were created at strategic points for the benefit of imported Mexican laborers. On the two main ranches more elaborate towns were built, which included stores, schools, churches, office buildings, and company-owned homes for permanent employees and ranch officials. At the heart of the operation was created the town of Litchfield Park, which eventually evolved into one of the most picturesque company-owned towns in the West. Wide streets were planned, and they were lined with palms and other ornamental trees. The business section was planned by the company, and even though the company eventually got out of the store business, it continued to determine what kind of enterprises would be allowed in town. Substantial homes were built, yards were well landscaped, and an attractive resort hotel was later constructed for official visitors. Facilities at the "Wigwam," as it is called, include an eighteen-hole golf course, two swimming pools, shuffleboard and croquet, badminton and tennis courts, and riding stables.

Litchfield Park is still company owned, although many features of a non-company town now characterize it. Many tenants, for example, are not employees of the company, and an attractive private residential area is springing up just off company property. It is no longer dominated by the company in quite the same way as the traditional company town, but Goodyear still takes pride in helping maintain an attractive, stable community.

Climax—The Molybdenum Town

One of the most important minerals used in the manufacture of today's tough, heat-resistant steel is molybdenum. The state of Colorado produces 76 per cent of the world's supply of this rare product, and virtually all Colorado's production comes from Climax, the scene of an extraordinary mine high in the mountains of Lake County. Climax was once one of the largest company towns in the West and Colorado's most prosperous community.

Climax was founded in the 1920's by Climax Molybdenum Company. At its peak the town housed 2,500 inhabitants, and the company provided all community services, including the hospital. The town was only twelve miles from historic Leadville, but this was still too far, in the twenties, for employees to commute on the high mountain roads, especially in the winter.

As late as 1954 community facilities were still expanding at Climax. By this time, however, improvements in transportation had made commuting less difficult, and the desire for individual home ownership had lured some workers to Leadville. In 1957 the company purchased Westpark, a housing development outside Leadville, which had been created with the idea of selling homes to Climax workers. Finally, in 1960, the entire town of Climax, together with the Westpark development, was sold to the John W. Galbreath Company. Employees were then given the opportunity to purchase Climax homes and have them moved to Westpark for a down payment as low as two hundred dollars. New homes at Westpark were also sold to Climax workers, and the town of Climax was abandoned when company officials decided the time had come for eliminating the expense and paternalism of community ownership. It was in the interest of better employee-employer relationships, explained Edward Eisenach, resident manager of the Climax mine. Noting that the national trend was away from company-owned towns, he said, "It was our belief that our employees would respond favorably to a chance to own their own home in an area away from their place of work yet close enough to make commuting easy."[3]

A giant moving operation quickly got under way in which all homes were sold and transported to Westpark. Even dormitory units were sold and moved by dividing them each into three parts. Mining operations at Climax have continued to expand, but since the company town was no longer necessary it has been eliminated.

Trona—The Potash Town

For the purpose of producing potash, boric acid, and similar chemical products, several companies have established elaborate pumping and manufacturing plants to process brines drawn from beneath lake beds. In the early days of this century such plants required the building of supporting towns, for they were usually located in very remote areas. Examples of such towns include Cartago, California, which was operated at Owens Lake by the California Alkali Company from 1917 to 1932, and Westend,

---

[3] *The Denver Post*, July 31, 1960.

74

California, which was managed by West End Chemical Company from 1919 to the 1960's.

Trona, California, is the home of a large plant operated by American Potash and Chemical Corporation, although several other companies have preceded it in ownership of the plant and the community. The company's chief Trona-made products are potash, borax, boric acid, soda ash, salt cake, bromine, and lithium carbonate, all of which are produced from brines pumped from beneath the crusted bed of Searles Lake. The desert community of Trona has run the full scale of evolution from a rough-and-tumble labor camp, through the fully-owned, paternalistic company town, to the modern company-dominated but privately owned municipality. Its story, therefore, is particularly interesting as a pattern for the study of company towns in general.

Trona was founded at the beginning of the twentieth century, and its early days were somewhat typical of the rugged, womanless pioneer settlement. Most of the fifty or sixty men employed lived in tents, and Dr. H. R. Evans, who occupied the company's first tiny medical office in 1914, recalled later that it was a "poor weekend indeed" that they did not have at least a dozen fights.[4] In 1916 the first permanent residential building, Austin Hall, was completed. Since there were no families in Trona, the hall was primarily a living quarters for single men. It also contained the company offices, dining hall, mercantile units, pool hall, and the post office, which shared quarters with the barbershop.[5] Such were the humble beginnings of a town which later became a stable community of 4,500 people.

By the 1920's the infant town had begun to assume a somewhat more organized existence. A few families had moved in, and the town boasted a one-room school. In 1923 the company began a weekly paper, the *Trona Potash*. For more than thirty years, however, the town remained essentially a bachelor community, and as

4 *The Trona Argonaut*, January 29, 1948.
5 *The Searles Review*, April 3, 1958; *The Brine Line*, July, 1956, 10.

late as 1951 more than 75 per cent of the company's employees were unmarried.[6] The desert heat, the fact that few roads connected Trona with the outside world, and the minimal maintenance provided for company houses were not conducive to family-type living.

The switch away from company ownership in Trona is an excellent example of what has happened to many company towns in the West. It was also a milestone in the social history of Trona. Improved transportation facilities, the gradual development of family life in Trona, the development of the desert cooler, the high turnover of unmarried employees, and the desire of the company to stabilize its payroll by bringing in a higher ratio of married men all influenced the final decision to make the change.

The first move took place in 1946, when American Potash and Chemical Corporation organized the Searles Valley Development Company. Ten houses were soon built and sold to employees. So successful was this experiment that sixty additional homes were built and sold. In 1953 the decision was made to sell all company-owned homes in Trona, and within one year the sales were complete. Trona became a county service area of San Bernardino County. To facilitate the change-over, the company donated all existing street lights, fire-protection facilities, and other public installations. At the same time it began to sell its various commercial enterprises. First to go was the automobile service station, with the company agreeing to close down only upon being assured that new operators would give as good or better service. The new operators actually provided better service, and three other stations eventually were opened in Trona. The same pattern was repeated in the disposal of other businesses.

As a result of this general switch the many advantages anticipated by the company began to be realized. The rate of employee turnover went down, the accident rate dropped, labor grievances

6 "Switch Away from Paternalism Pays Off for Company, Workers, Town," *Chemical Week*, Vol. LXXXI, No. 20 (November 16, 1957), 88.

declined, friction that came with assignment of houses by the company was eliminated, and more capital funds became available for investment in money-making projects. In addition, the number of family men in Trona increased to about 75 per cent of the employees, practically reversing the former ratio between married men and bachelors. Today's Trona is a modern company-dominated but self-governing community of home owners.

An isolated community such as Trona will often develop a sort of provincialism which makes it difficult to break any long-standing tradition. This is illustrated, in part, by the naming of the new theater in 1948. Practically every enterprise in town, including the Trona Theater, used the name of Trona. The *Trona Argonaut* sponsored a contest to name the new theater soon to be erected. So enthusiastic was the response, reported this company-owned paper, that an extra week was required to judge the entries and award the prizes. When the "several hundred" entries had all been judged and people waited eagerly for the new name, the name chosen, of course, was "Trona." It only proved, commented the *Argonaut*, that "there is nothing new under the desert sun."[7]

A few generalizations may be drawn from the story of Trona which reflect the development of many company towns in Western America. First, the company town was a natural development when a single industry began to operate in an isolated section of the country. Second, the company, primarily interested in its business, at first provided only minimal facilities for its employees. Third, the company town was at first largely a bachelor community, with families coming only after improved conditions made it more conducive to family living. Fourth, housing, goods, and services were provided through company-operated enterprises. The net result, however, was a loss for the company. Fifth, with improved transportation facilities making better integration with surrounding communities possible, both the employee and the company saw many benefits in the move away from paternalism.

7 *The Trona Argonaut*, September 9, 1948.

Finally, the modern company town is a co-operative venture, with the company still providing some recreational facilities for its employees but having little to do with housing, sale of goods, or other commercial activities.

CHAPTER VI

Community Planning and Housing

THE VERY EXISTENCE of a company-owned town raises a variety of interesting social questions. How well was the town planned and laid out? What kind of housing did the company provide, and how well was it maintained? What were the general living conditions? Did the company-town dweller represent a particular "type"? What provisions were made for public health and general welfare? Did racial problems exist? What kind of social activity was there, and how far did the company go in providing social halls, clubhouses, etc? Did the company foster religious activities? Was there any "community spirit"? Finally, did the rather isolated locations of most company towns create any unusual or distinctive social problems?

If a person suddenly found himself in the middle of a company-owned town, he would have little difficulty identifying it as such, for certain general features usually stood out. First to be noted would be the standard, uniform architecture of the company-owned houses. In a prominent location, however, would stand a larger, more imposing structure: the home of the company manager or superintendent. It would be observed that the town seemed to center around a focal point where a store, community hall, school, and other public buildings were located. The company store usually dominated the group. It would be noted that the settlement had no "suburbs," or no gradual building up from a few scattered homes to a center of population. Rather, one would note the complete isolation of the community and the definiteness of its boundaries. Finally, it would be apparent that the existence of the community was completely dependent upon a single enterprise, because a mine, mill, or smelter would seem to dominate the entire scene. Looking at Hilt, California, for example, it would take little imagination for a romanticist to think of the lumber mill as a father spreading his protective influence over a completely dependent group of dwellings.

In spite of the foregoing, it would be impossible to discover a completely "typical" company town, and too many generalizations on the social aspects of the company town would tend to mislead. It is nevertheless important to consider certain of these aspects, pointing to similarities which most commonly exist as well as some of the essential differences between towns.

Community Layout

The layout of company towns naturally varied according to geographic location, period of time, and the conscientiousness of the company in community planning. Early communities tended to be more haphazard in their arrangement, many of them having grown from typical mining or lumbering camps with houses located wherever the builder happened to feel like settling, and the company coming in later to take over. Modern company towns are laid out in a planned and orderly fashion.

A "typical" company town would have its layout determined largely by it geographic location. If the terrain were flat enough, rectangular blocks could be platted when the property was first settled, and a uniform community could be built. Although it is often supposed that most coal-mining camps were simply unplanned arrangements of houses, by the 1920's most of the coal-mining communities in the United States were arranged along rectangular lines of survey and were characterized by wide streets and ample lots.[1] Hanna, Wyoming, where coal mining began in 1889, was apparently one of the earliest communities in that area

[1] Leifur Magnusson, "Company Housing in the Bituminous Coal Fields," *Monthly Labor Review*, Vol. X, No. 4 (April, 1920), 216.

in which real attention was given to community planning. Declares the official history of the Union Pacific Coal Company:

> The streets were laid out at the opening of the town with some-what more consideration than had been given in the majority of other coal towns. Instead of digging into the most convenient gulch bank to make a dugout home, or erecting a building on the most convenient spot, the builders laid out an orderly scheme of streets and alleys, containing two concentrations of buildings, one near each of the mines. The main street ran north of and parallel to the railroad. South of the tracks the buildings were called No. One Camp, and north of the tracks they were called No. Two Camp, although each was a part of Hanna.[2]

Even though many company towns consisted of a single residential section, there are numerous exceptions. Sometimes the towns were divided into two or more camps, like Hanna, in order to accomodate company operations. In other cases the irregular terrain demanded that a number of sections be constructed. In Rockport, California, for example, the lumber mill was built on an inlet from the ocean to facilitate the loading of lumber to be shipped by schooners. Immediately behind the mill were large wooded hills, and the town was built in the small canyon away from the mill. A single row of houses, dubbed "staff row," occupied one arm of the canyon, while the rest of the dwellings occupied the other.

In many places the geographic location of the mine, mill, or smelter made an orderly layout impossible, and the company town, therefore, simply followed the terrain. At Falk, California, for example, the Elk River Mill and Lumber Company began operations in 1884 and continued until 1937. The company's mill was situated in a narrow canyon, and the town sprawled all over the hills and the canyon, with the company store located near the mill. This layout was similar to that followed by many of the early

2 *History of the Union Pacific Coal Mines*, 115.

lumber-mill communities built in canyons near the center of logging operations.

At Morenci, Arizona, the location of the open-pit copper mine in very hilly country has led to the evolution of a rather interesting community. The older part of the town presents a random arrangement of streets winding up the mountains to various dwellings. The problem of finding enough flat territory upon which to build is illustrated by the site of the elementary school. The school faces a main road running into town. The playground, however, is located on top of the school building, but it may be reached, without climbing stairs, from the street running behind the building. The new housing areas of Morenci—"Plantsite" and "Stargo"—are built on hillsides which have been terraced by the company, each terrace consisting of a single row of houses and an access road. Considering the problem of location, these are exceptionally well-planned residential areas.

A special problem in community planning may be seen in places where the company might eventually mine or otherwise develop the area set aside for residences. The entire town of Ray, Arizona, for example, will eventually be abandoned as technological advances have made increasingly profitable the mining of low-grade copper ore. With the expansion of the open-pit mine the residential area must be eliminated. At both Morenci and Ajo, Arizona, Phelps Dodge is constantly expanding its pits for the same reason, and older sections of town are gradually being razed.

The location of residential areas immediately adjacent to the company's operations was naturally a benefit to the employee in allowing him to get to work quickly and easily. In some cases, however, the houses were located without thought for health and comfort, and problems occurred. Some coal-mining communities, for example, were located near coking ovens on hillsides which had been denuded by the noxious gases. In some cases it is reported that towns were located so that prevailing winds kept them constantly enveloped in smoke.[3] In California, part of the town of Davenport was built on the wrong side of the cement plant, and the wind from the ocean blew dust over the houses making the area dirty and undesirable as a place to live.[4]

Beautification Projects

The process of community planning includes not only the location of streets and houses but also provision for beautification. Here again policies varied with the company as well as with the period of time considered.

Early company towns were not generally planned with an eye to beauty. Streets were wide but unpaved. Lawns, trees, and other greenery were rare, and public parks were few. This was especially true in coal-mining communities. Rains, Utah, is one example of a coal-mining town which provided nothing to beautify the town or yards, the town appearing simply as a wide dirt road with shacks and unimproved yards on either side.[5]

Such communities, however, are by no means representative of all company towns, for some companies were very conscious of beautification projects in their original planning, while others gradually developed an awareness of this need and took steps to meet it. Hiawatha, Utah, located only a few miles from Rains, is usually described as a very attractive community, almost giving the appearance of a community of contented property owners. Lawns, trees, flowers, and gardens were all encouraged by special inducements from the company.[6] At Ajo, Arizona, a desert was transformed into an oasis when Jack Greenway, of the Calumet and Arizona Mining Company, obtained water by drilling a huge

---

[3] Magnusson, "Company Housing in the Bituminous Coal Fields," *Monthly Labor Review*, Vol. X, No. 4 (April, 1920), 216. This is a survey of company housing throughout the United States in general, but his generalizations are applicable to the Western states.

[4] Interview with Charles J. Bella, Santa Cruz, Calif., May 4, 1962.

[5] Interview with William Goldman, Los Angeles, Calif., June 24, 1961. Mr. Goldman had several pictures of the town to verify his description.

[6] Thursey Jensen Reynolds (comp.), *Centennial Echos from Carbon County*, 214.

well. Trees and grass appeared as Greenway made a conscious effort to beautify the town, and the spacious plaza in the center of the community was lined with colorful oleanders.[7]

Many companies went far to encourage town residents to beautify their yards by giving annual prizes for the most attractive lots and by furnishing trees and shrubs to any tenant who would plant them. At Hanna, Wyoming, for example, the Union Pacific Coal Company began in 1915 to encourage such activity, hauling in trees by the carload for those who would plant them. Prizes were also given for the best yards and vegetable gardens. By 1919 Colorado Fuel and Iron Corporation was taking definite steps to improve the appearance of its many communities. House lots had been fenced, streets graded, and trees planted, and tenants were given every encouragement to cultivate lawns and gardens.[8]

Housing

The owners of Western America's company towns varied considerably in the type of housing provided for their employees and in their maintenance policies. The outward appearance of company houses, for instance, included the drab, unpainted wood of Caspar and Westwood, California; the plain cement block of some of the coal-mining communities; the uniform red houses of Weed, California; the well-kept white homes of Bacchus, Utah; the multi-colored stucco dwellings of Tyrone, New Mexico; and the well-painted frame structures of present-day McCloud, California.

As a general rule, companies which painted their houses at all preferred to paint them all the same color, most often red or gray, thus adding to the drab uniformity of the dwellings. The policy of many companies gradually changed, however, as management became more conscious of public and community relations. Homes in McCloud, California, were once a uniform gray, but the policy was later adopted of striving for attractiveness by painting them a

[7] Arthur Train, Jr., *Ajo*, 15.
[8] *Colorado Fuel and Iron Industrial Bulletin*, Vol. IV (April 30, 1919), 9.

variety of colors. In order to avoid bickering, tenants were not allowed to choose their own colors. In Hilt, California, the homes originally were not painted, for only a short life was planned for the community, but the company finally adopted the policy of furnishing the paint and a compressed air sprayer, allowing tenants to paint their own dwellings and giving them a choice of colors.[9] Most modern company towns still functioning as such today have moved away from single-color uniformity.

Most companies attempted to provide comfortable living quarters for their employees, but economic considerations naturally kept them from providing more than the bare necessities. A typical floor plan might include a kitchen, living room, two bedrooms, and bath. Sometimes a porch would be provided, which when screened could double as an additional sleeping area.

Building materials were usually those which were most readily available and least expensive. Coal camps were constructed of wood, cement block, or crude brick, while lumber-mill towns without exception were frame.

Much debate has taken place concerning the adequacy of company housing in the camps of Colorado Fuel and Iron Corporation. In his book Beshoar described the company dwellings of the early 1900's as "houses and shanties, barren little homes that reared their weather-beaten boards above piles of ashes and tin cans."[10] Company periodicals, however, declared in 1902 that the company was spending thousands of dollars in renovation and that in the newer settlements all company houses were "model workingmen's dwellings, neatly painted, thoroughly sanitary, convenient and homelike."[11] A supposedly unbiased government commission in 1915 reported that "housing conditions for the miners are exceptionally well provided, and every camp that we saw appeared to be doing much for the comfort of its employees."[12]

9 Interview with Irene F. Tallis, Hilt, Calif., May 2, 1962.
10 *Out of the Depths*, 2.
11 *Camp and Plant*, Vol. I (March 1, 1902), 180.
12 "Report of the Colorado Coal Commission," *Monthly Labor Review*, Vol. II, No. 4 (April, 1916), 48.

If the truth were fully known it would probably be seen that coal companies provided only that which was essential to keep employees working, and that homes of the ordinary miner were very cheaply constructed. Foremen and managers had somewhat better houses. The following attempt by A. T. Shurick to describe the general United States mining camp of the 1920's probably reflects the typical attitude of large mining companies, including Colorado Fuel and Iron, toward employee housing:

> In the well-designed mining camp today, recognition is taken of these varying needs and houses built accordingly. First there will be a few substantial, well-built houses, equipped with modern conveniences throughout and comparable with the better type of modest town house, for the superintendent, clerical forces, doctor, store manager, etc. Next there is a larger group of similar houses along less pretentious lines for foremen, sub-foremen, and some of the preferred class of men such as the electrician, master mechanic, etc. The balance of the houses which go to make up the bulk of the camp will be divided roughly into two general classes. The first of these will be of a fairly substantial and well-built type, usually four or five rooms and equipped with running water and possibly a bath and inside toilet facilities. This house is designed for the more permanent miners who appreciate something of a better class and it is usually plastered inside and equipped with some extras, such as a porch, that tend to lift it above the next class below. The inferior houses are designed to meet the requirements of the lower class of improvident miners who would be indifferent to anything above the crudest type of house and probably abuse anything better. These houses may be built somewhat along the lines of the next class above, but would be finished with wood ceiling inside, have outdoor toilets, and be dependent on an outside spigot for its water supply.[13]

No mention is made of how it was determined who were of the "lower class," but in the West it was usually the nonwhite and foreign elements who were so designated.

13 *The Coal Industry*, 312–13.

In the 1920's a survey of company houses in coal-mining communities throughout the United States revealed that 95 per cent of the houses were constructed of wood. Over two-thirds were finished outside with weatherboard, usually nailed directly to the frame with no sheathing or, sometimes, with paper sheathing. Composition paper was used for two-thirds of the roofs. Foundations were generally of posts, and no cellars were included. Most houses, except the poorest "shanties," had porches. Inside finish consisted of wood sheathing for half the houses and plaster for an additional 38 per cent. In the supplying of utilities, 13.8 per cent had running water, 2.4 per cent had bathtubs, and 3 per cent had flush toilets inside. A water system of some sort existed in only 49 per cent of the communities, and 66.3 per cent had electricity or gas.[14]

If the figures given above held generally true in the West, the "model workingmen's communities" described by some zealous company spokesmen left a good deal to be desired. On the other hand, company towns in the West were newer than most of the coal towns studied in this survey, the majority of which were located in the Eastern coal fields. In a less extensive survey in 1916 by the *Monthly Labor Review*, one large company operating twelve camps in Colorado and Wyoming reported that 74 per cent of its houses were of frame construction and 83 per cent were weatherboarded. Pebbled-ash was used for finishing 17 per cent of the houses, and 10 per cent were built of plain cement block. Colorado Fuel and Iron, furthermore, declared in 1919 that it had been making steady improvements in housing conditions. All the unsightly and unsanitary "squatter" shacks built by individuals had been removed from the camps, the report continued, and the company was then in the process of gradually replacing the oldest company-owned shacks with more modern homes, most of them built of brick or cement block. As far as sanitary conveniences were concerned, however, the 1916 survey checked 1,214 company dwellings in Colorado and Wyoming and found that none of them

14 U.S. Coal Commission *Report*, Vol. III, 1429–30.

had inside toilets. Of 642 other mining communities in Arizona, Colorado, and New Mexico, 45 per cent had inside toilets.[15]

In the early part of this century a number of model coal-mining communities were constructed in which the companies gave definite attention from the beginning to much-improved housing conditions. Such a town was Spring Canyon, Utah (originally named Storrs), begun in 1912 by the Spring Canyon Coal Company. Here the homes were substantially constructed of sandstone. Water, sewerage, and other modern conveniences were available in most of them. Other such Utah towns included Keetly, Hiawatha, and Standardville.[16]

In the lumber country, company houses were always constructed of wood. The typical small mill town usually consisted of houses with two bedrooms, kitchen, and living room, although more elaborate quarters were provided for management personnel. The earliest houses built were less comfortable than those which came later, but the average resident of a lumber-mill town seemed to be comfortable and satisfied with the facilities. The newer houses in Korbel, California, were described by a long-time resident as "very nice," each having five rooms and a bath, and renting for eighteen dollars a month.[17] Houses in many mill towns which have long since disappeared seem to have been well built. The last house erected in Newburg, California, for example, went up in 1912. The town disappeared, but fifty years later the house, still in good condition, was owned and occupied by the daughter of the original resident.

As a general rule, company towns in operation today boast of living quarters comparable in every way to the average home in other small communities. Water, sewerage, electricity, and gas are

15 Magnusson, "Company Housing in the Bituminous Coal Fields," *Monthly Labor Review*, Vol. X, No. 4 (April, 1920), 218–19; *Colorado Fuel and Iron Industrial Bulletin*, Vol. IV (April 30, 1919), 9.

16 Jesse William Knight, *The Jesse Knight Family*, 70; A. L. Murray, "Welfare and Safety in Connection with Mining in Utah," *The Mining Congress Journal*, Vol. XI, No. 10 (October, 1925), 478.

17 Letter from Ed C. Morrison, Hornitos, Calif., May 27, 1962.

supplied, regular maintenance is performed, telephone service is available, and the modern necessity of television is usually accessible through cable service.

Rental

Rental charges for company houses have always been low and frequently have served as an added inducement to live in an isolated area. In most cases rental charges were, and still are, deducted from the employee's pay check.

In the coal fields of Colorado and Wyoming in 1916, rent varied from $5.00 to $18.00 a month, with 78.5 per cent renting at less than $9.00. Rent usually included water. In camps where electricity was available charges for this service ranged from thirty-five cents a light per month to $3.00 a house. It was common to base rent payments on the number of rooms in the dwelling. Tenants at Madrid, New Mexico were charged $2.00 a room per month for an ordinary house, including coal for heating and cooking. An extra charge of fifty cents a drop was added for electric lights. In Climax, Colorado, rent varied from $5.00 a room per month for log cabins to $12.50 for steam-heated houses until 1957, when charges were raised to a minimum of $6.75 and a maximum of $14.75. An extra charge of $2.50 a month was made for an attached garage.[18]

Modern company towns naturally charge higher rates. Homes at American Smelting and Refining Company's little community of Silver Bell, Arizona, rent for $45.00 a month for two bedrooms and $55.00 for three bedrooms. This includes all utilities. In Scotia, California, the Pacific Lumber Company charges $60.00 a month for a three-bedroom home with garage, electricity, water, and garbage collection furnished. Even these rates, however, seem modest when compared with modern wages and with charges in other communities for comparable facilities.

18 Magnusson, "Company Housing in the Bituminous Coal Fields," *Monthly Labor Review*, Vol. X, No. 4 (April, 1920), 221–22; Oscar Huber letter; *Moly Mountain News*, Vol. VIII (December 3, 1956).

Maintenance

Upkeep and appearance of individual homes often depended not only upon company policy but also upon the character and attitude of the employee himself. The report of the Coal Mines Administration's medical survey of 1946, for example, made the following comment concerning housekeeping in coal-mining areas:

> And the incessant dirt, a native blend of coal dust from the tipple, smoke from the railroad, dust from the roads, sand, grime, and acrid fumes from the burning slag heaps, permeates and clings tenaciously to the structures and furnishings of houses and to human bodies. It takes will power, determination, and persistence on the part of the miner's wife to hold her own in this unending struggle, particularly in the camp where the houses may be akin to sieves. Many housewives give up after years of fruitless battle. Many, without any conception of better standards or training in homemaking, never try, even where the conditions in their favor are of the best. Others, spurred by self respect, pride, and devotion to their families, maintain their homes and care for their house-holds with a zeal that is limited only by their energy. Their housekeeping and homemaking are models of excellence, regardless of the shabbiness or attractiveness of the house structure itself.[19]

The report included many contrasting photographs illustrating the last point, but it indicated also the existence of a general correlation between good maintenance policies by management and good housekeeping.

That poor living conditions were often largely caused by the habits of a poor class of people is seen in one long-time resident's account of Sunnyside, Utah. Apparently rather prejudiced against the "foreign element," in her own mind she had justified that feeling:

> At one time, about 1915, when Sunnyside was booming its

[19] "The Coal Miner and His Family," Supplement to U.S. Coal Mines Administration, *A Medical Survey of the Bituminous Coal Industry*, 24–27.

greatest, a few of these southern European immigrants lived in New Town next door to us. They hollowed out one side of the foundation of their house and installed several hogs. The smell was awful. Complaining neighbors were responsible for them being ordered to get rid of them. They butchered them on the kitchen floor, and when the lady of the house decided to clean the entrails to stuff them with sausage, she tied one end of them securely to the faucet of the only water hydrant in the neighborhood and turned on the water. . . .

Dr. Dowd told me a story about a family of these immigrants. He was called in to attend a very sick woman. He opened the front door and chickens flew in all directions. Before he reached the door of the room where the sick woman lay near death, he had to drive several milk goats out of the way. To cap it all, she had a rabbit warren under the bed. It did not take the doctor long to make her husband understand he had to clean up the mess immediately.

When Standardville was built the Standard Coal Company built a very modern town. Every house had its bathroom. Within two years they had to remove most of the bathtubs from the houses, and from all the houses they rented to these immigrants. They clogged up the plumbing by using the bathtubs to scald their hogs at butchering time.[20]

While this is obviously an extreme example, it nevertheless illustrates the point that the appearance and upkeep of company houses depended upon employee attitude as well as company policy.

Frequent reports have stated that since foreign groups were not accustomed to living standards as high as those of American workers, they were given less desirable living quarters in the first place. The American Indians have been treated similarly. Education and exposure to modern standards, however, seem to improve younger generations. At Ajo, Arizona, the Phelps Dodge rental

[20] Lucile Richins, "A Social History of Sunnyside" (Utah Historical Records Survey, March, 1940), typewritten MS filed at Utah State Historical Society, Salt Lake City, Utah, 10–11.

agent recently began an interesting experiment. He conducted a survey of the town's Indians to determine how well they took care of their living quarters, rating them as good, fair, or poor. Most tenants were rated poor, but it was noted that the younger generation rated higher than their elders. Feeling that the younger people were beginning to demand better things, the company began to move those who rated highest into new and much better homes. If the experiment works, more will be allowed to move into such homes as the older section of town where they now live is gradually eliminated.[21]

Bachelor Quarters and Private Housing

In addition to the family living units considered above, every company town provided a hotel, boardinghouse, or cabins for single men. In companies with several camps, a single boardinghouse organization often extended from a central location to the other camps. At Midwest, Wyoming, the boardinghouse fed seven hundred single employees at the central camp and extended its organization to include six outside camps. The boardinghouse at the home camp also served as a hotel for teachers and for people traveling through. The boardinghouse was large enough to employ 120 people, including a traveling chef, head chef, matrons, cooks, bakers, and office employees.[22] At Climax, Colorado, the Climax Molybdenum Company owned a hotel and dining room which provided for 425 unmarried miners, construction workers, and mill hands. These were operated by a private contractor, but the company insisted upon good quality food and guaranteed a profit to the catering contractor. Employees paid $2.60 a day for board and lodging.[23]

Individual employees frequently were allowed to build their

21 Interview with Ted Shelton, rental agent, Phelps Dodge Corp., Ajo, Ariz., March 23, 1962.

22 *The Midwest Review*, Vol. VI (November, 1925), 17.

23 "A Salute to Climax Molybdenum," special supplement to *Empire*, the magazine of *The Denver Post*, Sunday, May 23, 1954, 37.

own shacks on company property leased to them at one dollar a year. As a general rule, company housing proved to be superior to that built by individuals, and most companies which remained very long at a particular location tried gradually to eliminate private housing from company property.

CHAPTER VII

Human Welfare

L IFE IN THE TYPICAL COMPANY TOWN differed little from that of any other small and rather isolated American community. Entertainment was of the homemade variety, with dancing, baseball, and school activities providing the main community recreational program. News and gossip traveled fast, and everyone seemed to know the business of everyone else in town.

In some ways, however, company towns were distinctive. Community recreational facilities were provided and maintained by the company, company participation in special holiday celebrations was not unusual, and company control of health and welfare facilities was almost universal. Since residents of company towns paid no taxes and had no elected government, it fell the lot of the company to construct and operate community facilities which a city government might otherwise have provided. The owners of company towns, therefore, found themselves engaged not only in business, but also in full-scale social programs, including health and welfare, recreation, religious activity, racial problems, and education.

The Problem of Isolation

Company towns frequently were located in remote areas that had little regular contact with the outside world, but this very isolation was in some cases an advantage. Employees had few places to spend their money, for example, and therefore often saved enough to purchase homes in other communities upon retirement. As far as recreational activities were concerned, the most remote company towns were usually those with the most company-provided facilities. In addition, many of these isolated communities, especially in the lumber areas, were ideally located with respect to natural facilities. Hunting, fishing, hiking, and winter sports were all readily available and often within walking distance of town. Isolation, therefore, was not always the disadvantage one might suspect.

The problem of providing goods and services not available through the company store was usually taken care of by permitting outside merchants to come in on a periodic basis. Valsetz, Oregon, is still an isolated company town, and here the company allows grocery, laundry, and other service trucks to come over the mountains from Dallas, Salem, and other communities. Some companies used to allow the use of their trains and stations to individuals who wanted to bring in supplies from other towns, although such privileges were given only when the company did not demand that all trading take place in or through the company store.

Provisions for Health and General Welfare

Among the most pressing problems arising from isolation was the need for medical and hospital care. The extent of this care naturally varied with the size and location of the town. In some instances only a nurse was provided, and cases which she could not handle were taken at company expense to hospitals in other towns. In other instances elaborate medical and hospital facilities were provided at the town, and company physicians, dentists, and even optometrists were on the payroll. Companies generally deducted one or two dollars a month from their employees' wages to help pay for these services, but in most cases the company hospital or dispensary still operated at a loss. Such fringe benefits are still among the advantages of company-town living, even though the monthly deduction is somewhat higher.

In some early towns the owners did not immediately begin to provide medical services. Local managers sometimes found themselves in the unenviable role of caretaker of all community needs, including that of doctor. A rather humerous account is related by the foreman of the early coal-mining camp of Cumberland, Wyoming. The epidemic occurred in the spring of 1901:

> The majority of my bunch of huskies took ill, all in the space of a few days, and they were real sick. I had a hunch that a contagious disease was prevalent, but I could not figure out the trouble. . . . My brain was fast becoming scrambled in trying to associate symptoms with anything I'd known, when an old fellow named Ned Larkin came into the office, and as Ned was plentifully pock-marked, it dawned on me that the solution was stamped on Ned's face. Questioning him as to the symptoms, I found they checked fairly well with those of my patients, so we booked the disease as smallpox. We were advised that the only sure cure was good whiskey, applied liberally both internally and externally. I ordered a ten-gallon keg from Kemmerer, and Ned, being immune, was placed in charge of the sick. In the meantime practically the whole population of the camp had gone to their bunks, but by liberal applications of whiskey, plus Ned's experience, we had in a short time the upper hand, with very few of the boys bearing marks from the disease. The pile of whiskey requisitions written looked as though each patient took a daily bath in that delectable fluid, but as we came out without any serious results there were no regrets. Ned's requisitions would generally read: "Please deliver to 'hospital' one gallon Old Hickory, cured in wood, for bathing Swedes."[1]

In contrast to these primitive methods, many companies developed elaborate and well-run systems of medical care. The Industrial Medical Plan of the Midwest Refining Company cost the employee only one dollar a month for which he and his family were entitled to all normal hospital and medical services, including X rays and operations. An extra fee of thirty-five dollars was charged for maternity cases.[2]

[1] *History of the Union Pacific Coal Mines*, 133.
[2] *The Midwest Review*, Vol. VII (January, 1926), 26.

The Colorado Fuel and Iron Corporation also made medical services a regular part of its operations. Some criticism was levied against the performance of these services, however, as reflected in an anti-company report on the 1914 strike:

> Evidence is abundant that the system of company hospitals and company doctors offered just cause for grievances. At Sunrise, Wyoming, where the Colorado Fuel and Iron Co. operates an iron mine, the company doctor acted with shocking brutality and carelessness in his treatment of miners and their families, according to the impressive testimony of the Reverend Daniel McCorkle, pastor of the Sunrise church. Not only that, but the company permitted him to deduct fees arbitrarily fixed by himself from the wages of employees before those wages were paid, these fees being for services not covered by the regular fee of $1.00 per month.[3]

In spite of such adverse comments, it should be recognized that Colorado Fuel and Iron at least made reasonable efforts to provide for the general health of its towns. In 1902 it was reported that a physician was located in every company camp, that water, streets, and houses were inspected regularly for sanitary conditions, and that doctors lectured to school children on sanitary habits.[4] By 1917 dispensaries had been erected in many camps and were planned at several others, and the company's main hospital at Minnequa was using the most modern methods. Oculists and dentists were also on company payrolls.[5]

An idea of the not-too-sanitary conditions which prevailed in some early mining towns is given by a long-time resident of Sunnyside, Utah:

> The milk supply of Sunnyside came from the Big Spring Ranch. Each forenoon the milkman came around, driving a lean hungry looking horse hitched to a light wagon which contained several

3 West, *Report on the Colorado Strike*, 73–74.
4 *Camp and Plant*, Vol. I (March 1, 1902), 180–81.
5 *Colorado Fuel and Iron Industrial Bulletin*, Vol. II (July 31, 1917), 5.

five-gallon cans of milk. We would go to the side of the wagon and hold up a lard bucket, pan, or some other container, and say, "I'll take a quart today" or "I'll have two quarts today please" and he would remove the lid of a can (which served as a quart measure) fill it with milk and pour it into our container. Sometimes the can was not too clean. Often his hands were not too clean. In winter he generally had a bad cold and then he wiped his nose on his sleeves. But [the system] had its advantages.[6]

No adequate survey has been taken of such sanitary procedures as water inspection, garbage collection, sewage disposal, etc., although it appears that most companies supplied these safeguards and procedures, especially when a doctor lived in the town. Again, the coal towns of Colorado have been criticized most severely in this area, with a wide variety of conditions, from substandard to highly acceptable, apparently existing. In 1919 a survey of the frequency of garbage collection in coal towns of Colorado and Wyoming was attempted, but only a few towns responded. One community reported daily collection. Another reported semi-weekly collection, but twelve other towns were operated by the same company, and it was assumed that the same frequency prevailed in these. One town reported monthly collection, while others simply reported "when necessary."[7] In the matter of sewage, it appears that most early camps had rather poor facilities, some of them even relying upon open ditches running through town. Around the 1920's, however, when model company towns were springing up, adequate sewerage systems began to be planned and installed.

Recreation and Social Activity

The game of baseball was a great pastime in the company town, especially in the early decades of this century. Nearly every community had its baseball diamond, and competition with other

---

[6] Richins, "A Social History of Sunnyside," 4.

[7] Leifur Magnusson, "Sanitary Aspects of Company Housing," *Monthly Labor Review*, Vol. VIII, No. 1 (January, 1919), 296.

towns in the vicinity ran high. Management and labor alike were interested in the success of the local team, and it was not uncommon for companies to put a few professional players on the payroll for the ball season. Ordinarily these players did little work for the company; rather, they spent their time improving the town team.

Most companies provided not only ball diamonds but also many other recreational facilities. In some cases it took a long time, but most long-lived company towns eventually acquired excellent community facilities. Company-built recreation halls which could be used for community dances as well as private parties were standard items in nearly every town. At Morenci, Arizona, a swimming pool, playgrounds, tennis courts, and a new baseball diamond have all been completed since 1940. At Scotia, California, the Pacific Lumber Company provides an elaborate summer recreational program for youngsters in the town. A special activity is the building of a large swimming pool in the river each summer and hiring professional life guards to teach swimming. It is a popular and well-organized program.

In larger towns it was customary for the company to encourage various fraternal and social organizations. Lodge halls were usually provided, either in connection with the community recreation hall or as separate buildings. These organizations also helped in providing much of the town's entertainment. Boy Scout organizations and other youth groups also were frequently sponsored.

The volunteer fire department, though not peculiar to company towns, was often a source of social activity. In McCloud, California, for example, the company provided a well-equipped social center at the fire station, and the fire department frequently sponsored card parties, dinners, and other activities. In Westwood, California, a Firemen's Club was formed, and the clubhouse was furnished with pool tables, baths, piano, phonograph, etc., for the exclusive use of the volunteer firemen. Each month an entertainment and supper was held. The company helped cover expenses with a monthly allowance to the fire department as well as making a payment for each alarm answered. As an auxiliary to the Firemen's Club the Firemen's Band was organized. All members of the band were workingmen, except the director, who was employed just for that purpose by the company. Both classical and jazz music was played, and the club was in demand in many places in Northern California.[8]

Several companies took pride in providing special community activities on national holidays. Madrid, New Mexico, was widely noted for its colorful Christmas celebration every year. Phelps Dodge Corporation still sponsors annual Christmas parties in Morenci and Ajo where Santa Claus makes his appearance and all children receive gifts. Some companies have had traditional Independence Day picnics, and others have held regular community parties on other special days.

Organization of community recreational activities did not necessarily rest with management alone. Frequently a community council or an employee's club was formed to plan and co-ordinate community activities. Various fund-raising projects might be carried out, and the company usually donated financially to the community recreational fund.

In the smallest towns, and in those which were only temporary, these activities were not as well developed. Evidence seems to indicate, however, that residents in the majority of the West's company towns were well taken care of as far as recreational opportunities were concerned.

Religion

The owners of company towns were willing not only to permit religious activity but, in many cases, to encourage it. For some small towns which were less isolated than others, religious needs could be taken care of in nearby communities. In other places the companies often built the churches and even went so far as to pay

8 Frank E. Graham, "Complete Motor Fire Department Protects California Mill," *The Timberman*, Vol. XXII, No. 3 (January, 1921), 98.

at least one minister. When the town was too small or could not afford the services of a full-time minister, permission was given for visiting clergymen to hold services in community halls, schools, etc. In at least one lumber town the company gave the minister part-time work in the mill when his flock was unable to support him.

Companies often went a long way to help in the erection and support of various churches. At Hanna, Wyoming, the Union Pacific Coal Company donated land and material for the construction of a Methodist-Episcopal church in 1891. At McCloud, California, the McCloud River Lumber Company built the community church, furnished a home for the minister, and gave him a small subsidy. The Baptist, Catholic, Episcopal, and Mt. Zion Baptist (colored) churches also have buildings in McCloud. At Dawson, New Mexico, Phelps Dodge Corporation provided a home and other subsidies for a Protestant minister. Here, however, most of the people were Catholic, and the several priests fitted well into the life of the community. Umpiring at baseball games was one of their usual tasks.

In the coal fields, Colorado Fuel and Iron Company had Protestant ministers on its payroll to serve many of its far-flung camps. Charges have been made that these pastors were not permitted to criticize company activities or to speak against policies supported by the company, but little evidence is available to substantiate such claims. Company publications, in fact, report that in several communities church buildings were erected by the company and that John D. Rockefeller, Jr., made it a specific condition that neither he nor the company should assume any control or responsibility over their management.[9] All in all, it appears that church activity in the company towns was a normal and healthy part of community life.

Diversity of Race and Nationality

A varied mixture of races and nationalities could be found in

9 *Colorado Fuel and Iron Industrial Bulletin*, Vol. II (October 31, 1916), 6.

many company-owned towns and camps. In the coal fields, for example, many workers were European immigrants who on their arrival in the United States had come directly to the company towns. While they did not settle exclusively in these communities, a report of the Coal Commission in 1923 suggested that the company town had a particular attraction to them. Said the report: "It is only in sections which have a large portion of foreign born that relatively large numbers of mine workers are found living in company communities when normal communities are within a practicable distance."[10] Undoubtedly one reason for this was the fact that the immigrant usually arrived almost penniless, and the paternalistic situation in the company town immediately gave him a home as well as credit in the company store. In lumber towns, Scandanavian and Italian workers seemed to be prominent, and in the copper towns of Arizona and New Mexico, a significant portion of the population were Mexican and Indian workers.

Racial segregation as well as separation according to national origin appears to have been common in company towns, and even in the 1960's, Negroes, Mexicans, and Indians often lived in separate sections of company towns where substantial numbers of their races were employed. When the town of Gamerco, New Mexico, was built in 1921, the company made definite plans for racial separation. A company spokesman explained the policy this way:

> One of the features to be considered in this field is the diversity of races. In addition to the usual nationalities common to the average mining camp, we find the Mexicans in large numbers and the Navajo Indians ranging in number from 1 to 5 per cent of the total. The Mexicans prefer to live in more or less segregated quarters, and a Mexican village has been started somewhat apart from the main camp. The Navajos build their own "hoogans" and the solution of their housing problems does not rest on the mine owner.[11]

10 U.S. Coal Commission *Report*, Vol. III, 1426.
11 Cooley, *Story of a Complete Modern Coal Mine*, 28.

102

Gamerco seems to be representative of the general pattern in mining communities. At Ray and Hayden, Arizona, special sections of town were set aside where Mexican workers could build their own homes. At Morenci, Mexican workers still live in a common section of town, very largely because of the natural tendency for racial groups to want to stay together. In the early history of Morenci there was segregation in schools and in social activity also. The Morenci Club, for example, was not open to Spanish Americans for many years, although a Spanish-American club existed for their benefit.[12] In recent years this situation has been changed. At Ajo the older section of town near the mine has become a regular Indian village, housing the Papagos employed by Phelps Dodge.

Residents of some company towns separated not only along color lines but also according to national origin. In Dawson, New Mexico, for example, different European national groups tended to live in separate sections of town. The problems of language and diverse social customs largely accounted for this, and apparently no great animosities existed between the various groups living in Dawson. This, of course, is a situation which is seen in many American communities with diverse national groups and should not be attributed to the company town in particular.

An idea of the variety of nationalities in the coal fields in the 1920's is seen in a report of the United States Coal Commission. Sixty per cent of all workers in the bituminous fields were reported as "native born whites." Eight per cent were "native colored," while the remaining 32 per cent came from outside the United States. In Wyoming the Union Pacific Coal Company reported in 1938 that 1,400 of its 2,366 miners were American. At least thirty-two additional national or racial groups were reported, however, the most prominent of which were English, Italians, Austrians, Finns, Greeks, and Slovakians.[13]

12 Watt, "History of Morenci," 104–105.
13 U.S. Coal Commission *Report*, Vol. III, 1422; *History of the Union Pacific Coal Mines*, 163–64.

The mixture of such diverse nationalities naturally created problems of communication, and some companies tried to do something about it. Colorado Fuel and Iron Corporation, for example, was acutely aware of this problem. *Camp and Plant*, a periodical for employees, usually included short articles in German, Spanish, and Italian. The company further attempted to stimulate American patriotism and citizenship in the coal camps by providing special instruction in English, American history, and government.

Schools

A company which owned an entire town had good reason for taking particular interest in the public schools, primarily because it was the largest taxpayer in the county and therefore had a vested interest in the schools. As a general rule the companies seemed to recognize the need for good education, and many of them took great pride in their schools. The schools were important not only as educational institutions but also as centers of community life.

Companies had various ways of promoting and supporting education. In early days some firms went so far as to build the school and hire a teacher. Usually, however, the company would work with the county school board. A company representative often served on the board, and it was not difficult to get company-approved policies adopted. School buildings were often erected by the company and later sold to the school district at a very nominal price.

In order to attract teachers to isolated communities, some companies still provide living quarters for them. In the Phelps Dodge towns of Morenci and Ajo, for example, single teachers live in special units constructed for them, and married teachers may rent low-cost company houses at the same rate as company employees.

Although Colorado Fuel and Iron apparently had good relations with local school officials, this company also sponsored its own kindergartens. In nearly every camp special facilities were provided, and a teacher was hired by the company for the benefit of the younger children. Support of schools thus played an important part in the over-all planning of the owners of company towns.

Community Spirit

The residents of many company towns developed a peculiarly loyal attachment to their communities. Even though the company itself was not always the object of great affection, there was something about the closeness of town life which developed an interesting and long-lasting community spirit. Residents of Dawson, New Mexico, for example, still look back with longing to the "Dawson Days," and whenever possible reunions and socials are held in the many areas to which they have scattered. In other cases, however, company-town residents showed no particular attachment to their communities, and the closing of a town was no cause for sadness. With the closings of coal towns this was particularly true.

Lumber-mill towns in general seemed to have some degree of community pride. Interviews with and letters from many residents of now extinct mill towns reveal a sort of nostalgia which indicates that they liked the whole atmosphere of company-town living. Wrote one man who worked in Korbel, California, for thirty-two years:

> I liked the town of Korbel to live and work in, and I liked the company to work for. Life in a company town is very much different from city or large town life. In a company town you get to know all of the people, and life is more informal. In a city sometimes you do not know your next door neighbor, and everybody is in a big hurry. In a company town you are more in the outdoors, and in the city you feel shut in.[14]

The Business Runs the Town

While all of the foregoing represents a sort of composite picture of the social aspects of the company town, it undoubtedly creates an image little different from that of other small Western com-

14 Ed C. Morrison letter.

munities. In the company town, however, there is a somewhat intangible overtone which seems to run through all phases of its life and is definitely connected with the complete dominance of a single company. It is a spirit which comes not necessarily as a conscious effort from the company, and it is not immediately perceivable or explainable by the employee. It is usually there, however, and seems only gradually to dawn upon the stranger as he visits the town. It might be described as the complete saturation by the company of the town, its inhabitants, and all its surroundings— the complete dominance of the business of the company in everything that is seen or talked about.

This intangible and almost inexpressible spirit can best be felt only by a trip to several company towns. In the very approach to the town one often begins to sense it. When visiting a typical copper town, for example, a person first drives through miles of barren desert, knowing that at the end of the narrow highway is the sole reason for the road's existence—a copper mine and its supporting community. Usually the first sign that he is approaching the town is a giant pile of overburden which has been removed from the open-pit mine. Next the visitor drives past the huge slag pile, which is naturally one of the identifying features of the smelter town. Next the towering stacks of the smelter loom into view, and finally, snuggled at the base of the smelter or scattered around the mine, the town is discovered. Usually signs along the road will identify the property as belonging to a particular company, and it is apparent that one is no longer on public property and that company permission is required for almost any kind of soliciting.

In the town, activities of the company seem naturally to become a part of community life and conversation. In communities adjacent to copper mines, dynamite blasts from the pit are taken as a matter of course. Every new company project finds its way into everyone's conversation, and when community activities are talked of, "the company" comes just as naturally into the discussion as a father would when a family is planning its activities. School projects

106

often center around company activities. The company store is the shopping center, and company-sponsored social and recreational activities provide the main social outlet.

In many company towns the whistle at the company plant is a regular part of community life. It not only determines the shifts, which in turn regulate family life, but it also tells time and provides a curfew. Company trains and company logging trucks become a regular and accepted part of the community, as did company-owned ships in the Pacific Coast's early lumber-mill towns. All this is only natural to the long-time resident, but the visitor cannot help observing that this illusive but veritable saturation by company business of everything is a very real and distinguishing social feature in the company town.

OWNERSHIP OF A COMPANY TOWN brought to top management a multitude of problems not normally associated with regular plant management and employee relationships. As the company became a landlord it inherited the thankless duties of home maintenance, settling quarrels between tenants, deciding between applicants for particular houses, collecting rent, and soothing the ruffled feelings of those who had grievances. In addition, the company assumed the full responsibility of government, being required to furnish all services ordinarily provided by elected city officials. The company alone was the town legislative and executive body. It handed down all rules and regulations and was responsible for putting them into effect. The company was responsible for maintenance of streets, community recreational facilities, and public utilities. Fire protection also came under its jurisdiction, as did a great deal of the responsibility of maintaining law and order. Provisions for all these governmental functions had to be made within the framework of company organization. The role of company management as landlord has been discussed in other chapters. Its function as a substitute for city government will be considered here.

The type and extent of town organization differed with the various companies involved. The common element in all communities was the fact that the local plant superintendent or manager was in complete charge of all aspects of management. In small towns he handled personally all community administrative matters, and he required little assistance in doing so. Maintenance crews worked directly under him, problems and complaints came directly to him, and he made all decisions with respect to housing.

In large communities the chain of organization became somewhat longer. At Valsetz, Oregon, for example, the resident manager is solely responsible for the town, along with all other company operations, but the specific assignment pertaining to community management is delegated to a townsite manager. Under him, other individuals are designated to supervise specific enterprises, such as housing, stores, recreational facilities, etc. Law enforcement is handled by a company employee deputized by the county.[1]

In the Phelps Dodge communities of Ajo and Morenci local branch managers are fully responsible to the company for the towns as well as all other operations. In each case the branch manager is charged with community planning and development, although company engineers and other interested departments participate. Here, it will be remembered, the expansion of the mine is a determining factor in community development, and the engineers are therefore much concerned. The day-to-day affairs of the community, however, are of little concern to the branch manager, as other departments are delegated various responsibilities. A rental agent is employed who handles all problems pertaining to housing. Maintenance is provided through the company's regular maintenance department, although the rental agent sets up schedules for house painting and other routine procedures. In each town the county provides deputy sheriffs, and the company also hires security police who are deputized by the county.

There has been no standard procedure for providing public utilities in company-owned towns. Frequently the company would furnish electricity and fuel free of charge. This was especially true in early company towns, before metering became common. Sometimes the company allowed private firms to furnish these services. In other cases subsidiary companies were formed. Such a company

---

1 Interview with James Bryson, general manager, Valsetz Division, Boise Cascade Corp., Portland, Ore., April 25, 1962.

is the Morenci Improvement Company, which is housed at the Morenci Hotel and provides water and electricity for the town.

A problem of human relations sometimes arose in connection with services provided by the company. At Hanna, Wyoming, the story is told of early difficulties involved in collecting charges due on unmetered electric lights. Residents were billed on the basis of the number and size of bulbs in the house at the time the company auditor came to check. When the auditor once knocked on the door of a Mrs. Miller and announced that he was going to check the lights, he could see inside that the drop cords were still swinging back and forth. "My God!" said Mrs. Miller in feigned dismay, "I was cleaning my house this morning and I broke every bloody light!" The town had no telephones, but somehow everyone had a way of letting his neighbor know that lights were being checked. The auditor, it is reported, did not find many light bulbs, but he saw a lot of swinging cords.[2]

The administration of Trona, California, is an interesting example of how one company functioned as combination landlord and government service agency. Here practically everyone, including doctors, nurses, barbers, store clerks, and police officers, were on the payroll of American Potash and Chemical Corporation. Services were operated under one of two regular departments of the company—the Village Service Department and the Mercantile Department.

Housing at Trona was the direct responsibility of the Village Service Department. In 1948 there were fifteen dormitories in the village, two of which were set aside for single women. Some eighty people were employed to make beds and do the janitorial work in these bachelor quarters. The department also maintained 387 houses, 76 family apartments, and 692 garages.

The Village Service Control Unit, which handled all record keeping for the housing units, had a deputy county clerk who also

[2] Henry Jones interview.

Phelps Dodge Company Store at Dawson, New Mexico. Although
neither the company store nor town still exists, for years the store
did a flourishing business in the coal fields of New Mexico.

"Boleta" Used at Tubac. This one was worth fifty cents.

Metal Tokens Used for Scrip at Wilark, Oregon. This "dummy money,"
as it was called, was accepted in the company store of Clark and
Wilson Lumber Company. The company issued tokens in
denominations of five, ten, twenty-five, and fifty cents
and one dollar.

Courtesy W. W. Clark

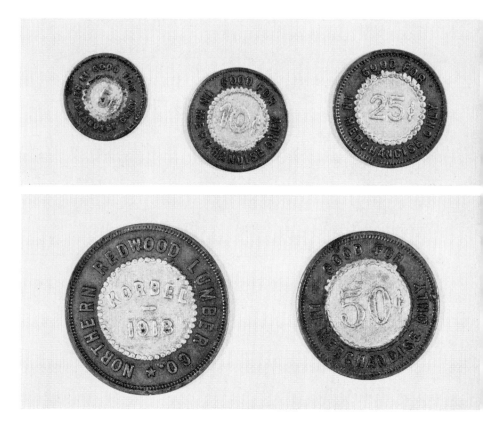

Metal Tokens Once Used for Scrip at Korbel, California.

Courtesy Simpson Timber Company

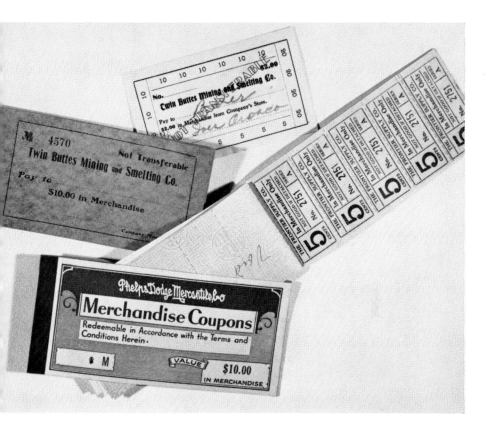

A Variety of Company Scrip. Scrip was issued in several forms, including punch cards and books of detachable coupons. Phelps Dodge Mercantile Company still accepts "merchandise coupons" in several of its stores.

Westpark and Leadville, Colorado. Westpark, made up of houses privately owned by employees of the Climax Molybdenum Company, was created when the company-owned town of Climax was sold. It is a new, modern housing development, created as a suburb of Leadville, and exemplifies the modern trend away from company-owned housing.

Courtesy Harold L. Potter

Silver Bell, Arizona. Located in the middle of the Arizona desert,
Silver Bell is a reminder that company-owned towns still are
necessary in some of the more remote areas of the West.
Owned by American Smelting and Refining Company,
the town is situated just three miles from the old
mining camp of Silver Bell which closed in 1928.

"A Dying Company Town"—Climax, Colorado. Climax is here shown after John W. Galbreath and Company had sold the homes and had begun moving them to the new housing area of Westpark.

Courtesy Harold L. Potter

acted as registrar of vital statistics. This unit thus became directly involved with county government and furnished a complete record for the township.

The Maintenance Division at Trona, part of the Village Service Department, had a direct effect upon the lives of the town's residents. It maintained a complete carpenter shop, plumbing shop, electrical shop, paint shop, and office-machine repair shop. A tenant with a broken window, clogged plumbing, or a broken doorstep needed only to call Village Maintenance in order to get it repaired. In short, everything around the home, even a burned-out light bulb, was taken care of by the company.

Other basic services at Trona included police and fire protection. Responsible for law and order on company-owned property was the Plant and Village Protection Section. All officers, although working for the company, were deputized by the San Bernardino County sheriff's office. The Trona Fire Department, under direct supervision of the company's Engineering Department, in 1948 included one fully trained chief and twenty-nine volunteer firemen. The company provided an elaborate alarm system and placed high-pressure water hydrants throughout the plant and village. Community police and fire protection in Trona, as in other company towns, was thus provided through a regular company department which simply extended its services to meet community needs.

Some Special Problems

Most problems of town management were simply problems in human relations, such as determining who got to live in which company house. The company superintendent nearly always was provided with the finest residence in town. Sometimes other dwellings would be graded according to job classification, and if a man received a promotion he also had the opportunity to move into a better house. At Ajo, Arizona, a point system is currently in use. Since there is a waiting list for company houses, the rental agent

111

assigns points based on date of application, length of employment, size of family, and job rating. When a vacancy occurs, the man with the highest number of points gets it.

A problem which sometimes occurs in connection with housing is what to do with retired workers and widows of former employees. According to the theory of company control, such people should vacate in order to make room for other workers. A question of propriety arises, however, when someone refuses to move. In 1962, for instance, three retired employees still lived in Scotia, California, refusing to abandon the town in which they had spent most of their lives. A company representative indicated that they had been given no specific period in which to move but that they would eventually have to leave even though the company had not yet attempted to force them out.[3]

That other companies were also charitable in this respect is seen in the history of Kennecott Copper's town of McGill, Nevada. In 1950 an acute housing shortage occurred because the widows of long-time employees had been allowed to continue living in company houses. The custom had begun during the depression when there were plenty of vacant houses. Instead of turning the widows out, the company built a widow's apartment unit for those who had no relatives or no place to go. Twelve moved into the new unit while several others left the community.[4]

Labor unions did not play a direct part in the management of company towns, for management usually refused to negotiate on such items as house rents, maintenance, etc. In some cases, however, the unions were indirectly involved because of their organization of the various town-service employees. The McCloud River Lumber Company, for example, signed three different contracts with the International Woodworkers of America: one for the plant,

3 Alden Ball interview.
4 Letter from D. K. Stark, industrial relations representative, Kennecott Copper Corp., Nevada Mines Division, McGill, Nev., June 6, 1962.
5 "Working Agreement between the McCloud River Lumber Company and Town Sub Local Union No. 6–64 I.W.A.-C.I.O. McCloud, California" (1953), 4.

one for the woods, and one for the town of McCloud. A 1953 agreement signed with the town sub-local recognized the union as bargaining agent for employees of the store, restaurant, hotel (including bakery), garage, and billiard room, as well as for carpenters, painters, plumbers, electricians, and the "town crew."[5] The contract established hours and conditions of work, rates of pay, seniority recognition, and all other agreements normally covered by unions. It also established a grievance committee known as the Town Committee. In this way unions might have some effect upon town management, although basic control remains in the hands of the company.

Among the many tasks assumed by company-town managers was that of keeping unauthorized peddlers and merchants out of their communities. In most towns where company stores operated, few if any other merchants were allowed to establish permanent facilities, although permission frequently was given them to solicit on certain days. Since the demise of the company store, it is still up to the company to determine which businessmen shall be allowed to install themselves in town. The company usually limits the number of firms which may be established and provides specific locations for them. Such control is justified in terms of space as well as a realistic consideration of the limited opportunity available to these businesses. In addition, many companies maintain a firm control over transient peddlers and solicitors, requiring them to obtain permits at the company office before entering the town.

Finally, it must be observed that a most frequent problem which came to those responsible for management of company towns was the fear of many residents that they would not get everything that was coming to them. "Whenever a house was improved," wrote a former director of Kennecott's Employee Relations Department at McGill, "the neighbor or one with a similar job would be sure to ask for the same repair. This problem was a constant headache."[6]

In summary, it is evident that to govern a company town was no

6 D. K. Stark letter.

simple task, even though it was only a minor part of total company operations. The problem of providing community regulations and services and, above all, the perplexities of human relationships made the successful management of a company town a distinctive challenge to scores of Western businesses.

CHAPTER IX

Economics, Politics, and Paternalism

Economic Considerations

THE COST OF BUILDING a "typical" company town is difficult to determine because there were so many variables.[1] Towns which evolved slowly must be considered differently from those which were specially planned and erected. The size of a town also affected the cost, as well as the amount of extra community services provided. Availability of building material was also an important factor, with lumber-mill towns obviously having a distinct advantage. Taking all these factors into consideration, it must simply be observed that the building of a town represented a substantial portion of the company's original investment in that property.

In 1914 Phelps Dodge Corporation began construction of a new mining town at Tyrone, New Mexico. Erection of houses, company office, railroad terminal, and community recreational facilities progressed simultaneously. By January 1, 1918, the company had completed and made available 163 dwellings. The table on the next page shows the amount of money invested, additional expenditure planned, and the amount received back from revenue-bearing investments.[2]

In addition to the expenses mentioned in the table, a company hospital had been erected at a cost of $75,000. If this is added to the "estimated investment when finished," it is seen that the company originally planned to invest well over $800,000 in the town-site alone, exclusive of the cost of the land. Still to be erected at the

1 Also, lack of direct access to corporate records has made this information difficult to obtain.
2 Table is based on Leifur Magnusson, "A Modern Copper Mining Town," *Monthly Labor Review*, Vol. VII, No. 3 (September, 1918), 281.

time this report was made was a clubhouse, library, and other community recreational facilities. A later source indicates that the final cost of the town was one million dollars.[3]

ANTICIPATED COSTS AT TYRONE, NEW MEXICO, 1918

Items	Amt. invested Jan. 1, 1918	Est. invested when finished	Net revenue rec. in 1917
Residences:			
Dwellings	$215,232	$250,350	$17,035
Garages (6)	1,085	1,200	28
House engineering	4,644	5,000	. . . .
Subtotal	$220,961	$256,550	$17,063
General Buildings:			
Store & warehouse	$172,837	$173,500	$20,622
Schoolhouse	76,532	83,000	1,176
Post Office	14,274	15,000	*
Bank, shop, and store	39,533	53,200	*
Subtotal	$303,176	$324,700	$21,798
Sundry improvements:			
Water system	$ 50,778	$ 51,000	$10,213
Light & power system	7,205	8,000	2,811
Roads & streets	37,360	38,000	†
Sewer system	13,698	16,000	1,913
Justice court	3,167	3,200	†
Engineering office expen.	18,396	20,000	†
Plaza improve.	13,019	14,000	†
Sundry expenses	1,784	2,000	†
Subtotal	$145,407	$152,200	$14,967
Total	$669,541	$733,450	$53,828

* Not reported.
† Nonrevenue-bearing investment.

It is important to note that in 1917 $53,828 had been returned from rentals, store, etc. This, combined with the fact that the hospital undoubtedly was losing money, and with future expenses

3 WPA Writers' Program, *New Mexico*, 418.

involved in town maintenance and repairs, indicates that it would have taken at least two decades for the original townsite investment to return to the company through these sources. The cost appears even heavier when it is realized that the Tyrone mines closed in 1921 and have operated only sporadically since that time.

No indication is given of the total cost of developing the Tyrone property, and it is therefore difficult to estimate the portion of the cost taken up by the company town. A more recent copper-mining town at Weed Heights, Nevada, was erected by the Anaconda Company in the 1950's as part of a total development expenditure of forty million dollars. If it is estimated that the townsite alone cost two million dollars (and this is undoubtedly very conservative in view of rising costs and the fact that Weed Heights has excellent houses and community facilities), it is seen that a company town could absorb at least 5 per cent of the original cost of developing a particular mining property.

Figures from a few additional towns will serve to give some idea of the relative economic significance of company towns in the over-all operations of particular firms. The 1911 balance sheet of the Weed Lumber Company, Weed, California, listed total assets of $4,862,751.20. "Tenement buildings" were valued at $142,252.80, while ranch lands and townsite property together were worth $86,088.32.[4] If ranch lands are considered as part of the town's support, approximately 4.7 per cent of the company's total assets were invested in the townsite and its supporting operations.

Weed Lumber Company's profit and loss statement for 1911 showed that gross income from the store, barbershop, hospital, company ranch, bar, boardinghouse, hotel, and rentals amounted to $67,646.48, or approximately 20 per cent of the gross income from all sources. The balance-sheet value of these same assets was $228,341.12. The income from this property, then, was approxi-

4 Weed Lumber Company, "Annual Report" (1911). With Weed Lumber Co. papers housed at Bancroft Library, Berkeley, Calif.

mately 30 per cent of its total value. If the figures for 1911 are representative of Weed Lumber Company's normal operations in that period, its investment would have been returned in less than four years. In this case it appears that the running of a company town was not a long-range liability.

Weed, however, was unusual. Although it was a company town, it was one of those communities in which private housing existed adjacent to company property, and employees were encouraged to build their own homes outside of town when possible.[5] Total investment in housing, therefore, did not reflect the total number of employees, as in the case of such towns as McCloud. In addition, the Weed Lumber Company did not invest any substantial amount in upkeep of company houses, spending only a total of $259.05 on repairs in 1911, most of which involved labor rather than supplies. A former general manager readily admitted that the town had "a lot of haywire houses," but candidly pointed out that the company was in the lumber business to make money, not to put money into new houses.[6]

In 1911 Weed Hotel earned only $1.98. It seems to have been normal for company-owned hotels, most of which were very luxurious, to break even or even to lose money. Hospital profit at Weed was listed at $2,563.71. This seems to be highly unusual in company towns, for almost all the hospitals lost money. At Midwest, Wyoming, for example, a 1925 report showed a net loss in the hospital of $4,366.39.[7] Phelps Dodge currently owns company hospitals in each of its communities and operates them at a substantial economic loss each year. Weed, therefore, does not necessarily represent normal company-town economics.

Town improvement was a continuing operating cost. In 1920, the year before Phelps Dodge acquired holdings of the Arizona Copper Company at Morenci, the latter company's cost statement

---

[5] Interview with J. M. White, former president, Long-Bell Lumber Co., Weed, Calif., April 20, 1962.

[6] *Ibid.*

[7] *The Midwest Review*, Vol. VII (January, 1926), 26.

for the year ending September 30 showed a total of $5,402.02 spent for town improvements. Since total costs were listed at $2,294,676.93, it can be seen that only about .2 per cent of this sum was eaten up by the town.[8] In later years, however, Phelps Dodge made heavy expenditures in town development. Between 1936 and 1957 the company spent over thirteen million dollars on housing alone.[9]

The owners of company towns which exist today have put substantial amounts into continued upkeep. Scotia, California, for instance, has regular maintenance schedules, and the houses are kept well painted and in good repair by the company. Relative cost figures are not available, but most managers consider their towns an economic loss as far as town operations alone are concerned. They hold on to them only out of an assumed necessity. The general manager of the Valsetz Division of the Boise Cascade Corporation reported that the company town of Valsetz, Oregon, cost the company $8,000 in the first three months of 1962.[10]

Another aspect of company-town economics is seen in the relationship of total employees working in the company's primary industry to the number working in other businesses. In other words, how many people and how much wage money does it take to provide supporting community services for the company town? In 1953 and 1954 John W. Leonard made such a study at Ajo, Arizona, under the direction of the Bureau of Business Research at the University of Arizona.[11] Although his conclusions apply only to one town, they are significant enough to mention briefly here.

Leonard used the term "basic" to describe the copper industry in Ajo, and all other activities were described as "non-basic." It

8 Arizona Copper Company, "Cost Statement" for the year ending September 30, 1920, in Arizona Copper Co. papers at the University of Arizona, Tucson, Ariz.

9 Phelps Dodge Corp., *Annual Report* (1957), 14.

10 James Bryson interview.

11 John W. Leonard, "The Economics of a One-Industry Town" (unpublished Master's thesis, College of Business and Public Administration, University of Arizona, 1954). Reviewed by L. S. Casaday in *Arizona Business and Economic Review*, Vol. III (December, 1954). The following material is based on the review.

was found that at any given time employment in the basic mining industry was from three to four times higher than employment in all other activities. In 1942, for example, employment in the basic field was 1,057, while non-basic employment was 257, for a ratio of 1 to .24. In 1952 basic employment was 1,220 as opposed to 422 in the non-basic fields, for a ratio of 1 to .35. To put it another way, it took from one-quarter to one-third of a worker in non-basic activities to support one worker in the basic industry.

With respect to wages, Leonard found that those employed in non-basic activities received substantially less than those who worked in the basic industry. It should be remembered here that in Ajo a number of private businesses are allowed to operate, in addition to the company store. In 1942 the non-basic workers received an average wage of $1,816, as compared with $2,697 in the basic industry. This was a ratio of 1 to .67. By 1952 the respective salaries were up to $3,221 and $5,487, for a ratio of 1 to .59.

Although the foregoing study is highly interesting and probably represents the trend in most large company towns, it should not be taken as final. Its validity has yet to be demonstrated through additional studies.

Some Political Aspects

Internal political activity was generally of little importance in the company town, primarily because very few towns were incorporated or had any form of elected government. The company managed everything, and usually there was neither necessity nor opportunity for residents to become involved in the problems of local government.

In terms of national politics, residents of company-owned communities showed only average interest. In 1960, for example, there were 2,227 registered voters in the four Morenci precincts, and 1,331 turned out to vote.[12]

12 Interview with J. A. Lentz, manager, Morenci Branch, Phelps Dodge Corp., Morenci, Ariz., March 14, 1962. Mr. Lentz had all recent voting statistics readily available.

120

Political-party division in company towns seems to have favored the Democrats, at least since the 1930's. The 1960 registration of Greenlee County, Arizona, in which Morenci provided nearly half the voters, showed 5,027 Democrats and 285 Republicans.

Although there is little evidence in recent decades to indicate that company pressure was effective in determining the way employees voted in national elections, in the early part of this century some such coercion most likely existed. A long-time, and sympathetically pro-company, resident of Hanna, Wyoming, reports that in the early days the town superintendent was always Republican, "and that was it, everyone else was." He told them how to vote and they voted that way.[13] Only after 1918 did things begin to change, and by 1924 the two major parties held equal power in Hanna. In 1928 the Democrats took the lead and remained thereafter the dominant party. One resident of Dawson, New Mexico, reported that in the 1932 election the company made every effort to induce its employees to vote for Hoover, but in the final analysis most of the town had voted for Roosevelt.[14] This seems to indicate that company pressure to influence national politics, when exercised at all, was not usually successful after the 1920's.

The owners of company towns were sometimes very effective in their control of local political affairs. Reference already has been made to the manner in which Colorado Fuel and Iron was accused of controlling elections for county sheriff.[15] In other areas companies worked directly with county sheriffs in appointing deputies for the town. At Hanna, for example, the deputy sheriff was always a regular employee of the company. A former resident of the company town of Cartago, California, reports that he once held the job of sheriff there "because the superintendent wanted me to have it."[16] He served without pay.

13 Henry Jones interview.
14 William Goldman interview.
15 See Chapter IV.
16 Interview with John W. Marshall, Calimesa, Calif., February 19, 1962.

It should not be assumed that there was any malicious intent on the part of all companies in their control of deputy sheriff appointments. It was, rather, simply a practical method of taking care of such law-enforcement problems as existed. In most fully developed company towns, it should be reported, few law-enforcement problems existed.

Since the company had a financial interest in public schools by virtue of its position as the only taxpayer in the community, it was only natural for owners of a company town to take special interest in school-board elections. It was common for the company to sponsor candidates for the county board of education as well as for local boards. Frequently the company superintendent was chairman of the local board, and always the company had much to say about school-bond issues and other school policies, but little if any malevolence seems to have been involved in this company control.

Paternalism

The word "paternalism" appears frequently in materials pertaining to company towns. Management, however, attempts consciously to avoid its use, for it connotes a type of company control destructive of personal liberty. Nevertheless it is a word which must necessarily be used in describing the company-owned community. As defined by Webster, paternalism is simply "a relation between the governed and the government, the employed and the employer, etc., involving care and control suggestive of those followed by a father; also, the principles or practices so involved."[17]

From the company's point of view, the privilege of living in a company town depended upon an individual's specific value, either as an employee or as a worker in some business directly contributing to the support of the community. The company seldom expected its investment in housing and other facilities to be returned through direct income. These features, rather, were considered as extra subsidies to the employee. The company therefore felt the

[17] *Webster's New Collegiate Dictionary*, 1953.

right to demand certain concessions from its town residents. If, in the early decades of this century, union organizers were trying to get a foothold in the town, the company was naturally unwilling to allow its property, including its houses, stores, etc., to be used for purposes which it considered inimical to its own interests. If an employee were discharged from the company, or if he resigned, the company claimed the right to take his house along with his job in order to make room for the man who would take his place. In Utah, for example, a strike in the winter of 1903–1904 resulted in the eviction of strikers. Many miners had been allowed to build their own homes on company land, and they were required either to sell these houses to the company by a given deadline or remove them from the property. Houses not sold by the deadline became company property.[18] If this was paternalism, it is clear that the prodigal son had a difficult time returning to his father's fold.

On the other hand, owners of many company towns have felt a positive responsibility toward their employees. Speaking of the fact that his company realized the direct effect it could have in the lives of workers at Valsetz, Oregon, a general manager remarked: "We keenly and genuinely feel our responsibility toward that which has been entrusted to us. We believe in the dignity of man and the worth of the individual."[19] He noted that company policy attempted to eliminate racial prejudice. It also promoted programs designed for the moral and physical improvement of its workers. Similar expressions were made by officials at many of the West's present-day company towns.

It might be argued that these glowing statements of good intent are simply the expression of company officials trying to counter past bad publicity. Selfish motives, it could be maintained, are behind all efforts to improve the attitude of the employee toward the company. Whatever the reason, it is true that company-town living today is a relatively easy life, and that the various paternal-

18 State of Utah, *Report of the Coal Mine Inspector for the State of Utah, for the years 1903 and 1904* (Salt Lake City, 1905), 67–71.
19 James Bryson interview.

123

istic projects of the companies involved have made isolation not the handicap one might suppose. It is not impossible to believe that a sincere benevolence was at least partly involved in the motives of some of the owners of the West's paternalistic communities.

The question of whether paternalism was good or bad for the individual has constantly been under debate and certainly cannot finally be answered here. Much of the answer, however, depends upon such factors as the attitude of the company toward its employees, the kind of individual worker involved, and the degree of company control or coercion exercised.

Many companies argue that the company town can be a positive good for both the worker and the company. At Climax, Colorado, for example, the company once experienced an exceptionally high employee turnover, indicating that living and working conditions were not attracting the permanent, stable worker which the company desired. Arthur H. Bunker, president of Climax Molybdenum Company, ordered a program of modernization and improvement, called the "Design for Man," in order to stabilize employment. In addition to better pay, the company provided more comfortable homes, provisions for health and safety, a good hospital, a modern school, and many other comforts of modern life, including television. By 1954 it was reported that employee turnover had slowed to a trickle, indicating satisfaction not only for the worker but also for the company.[20]

Additional evidence for the benefits of the company town is seen in the fact that many employees, while spending what to them was a satisfactory career working for the company, saved enough money to purchase homes in other communities when they retired. Inexpensive housing, low hospital bills, lack of need or incentive to travel far from home even on weekends, lack of need to commute to work, and good pay all combined to make life in the company town not only attractive but often constructive.

On the other hand, it is often observed that the paternalism of

[20] "A Salute to Climax Molybdenum," 37.

the company town stifled the initiative of the individual, was not really appreciated, and sometimes resulted in dissatisfaction and an unstable work force. Evidence is seen in the fact that employees frequently neglected their yards and houses, having learned to depend upon the company for everything. The pride of home ownership, it is argued, would improve the appearance of a community as well as the moral stature of the worker himself. When the town of Trona, California, was sold to residents, labor turnover went down, many former grievances between labor and management were eliminated, and residents developed an active, wholesome community spirit. In this instance the elimination of the company town seemed to benefit all concerned. Even after all the improvements made at Climax, Colorado, residents still seemed to appreciate the opportunity to own their own homes in their own community when Climax Molybdenum decided to eliminate the town.

The effect of company-town living upon the individual seems, in the final analysis, to depend not upon the degree of paternalism exercised by the company but, rather, upon the innate character of the individual himself. Frequently it is reported that homes standing side by side demonstrated both extremes of care and upkeep. An outsider who frequently visited Westwood, California, reports that homes which, by company policy, were crude and unpainted outside, were often very neat and comfortable inside, while a neighbor's home might be just the opposite, illustrating the differences in people.[21] The same thing was true in the coal fields, as reported by a 1947 medical survey report.[22] It is impossible categorically to declare that company-town living destroyed or undermined individual initiative and pride.

Those who would criticize the company-town atmosphere have at least one strong argument in an almost universal characteristic—

21 Interview with Emanuel Fritz, professor emeritus, School of Forestry, University of California, Berkeley, Calif., April 11, 1962.

22 U.S. Coal Mines Administration, *A Medical Survey of the Bituminous Coal Industry*, 27.

the tendency of company-town tenants to take advantage of the company in every possible way. "Where much is given more is expected" is a maxim well applied to the typical company-owned village. Since the company was supposed to take care of house maintenance, for example, many residents refused even to care for small items, feeling almost as if they had been cheated if they did some work which the company ought to have someone else do.

Describing the feelings of a typical coal miner at the end of a working day, a government survey team put it this way: "He wonders angrily why the 'boss' doesn't fix the foundations and the porch—he has complained about it so many times—and then he thinks that maybe, when he gets a chance, he'll fix them himself, even if it isn't right that he should do so."[23] A former company clerk from Hanna, Wyoming, reported on the many "gripes" he had to listen to, especially on housing: "If we did something for Mrs. Jackson, we could almost bet our last bottom dollar that the next morning Mrs. Tacalon, or Scarapelli, would be there wanting the same identical things, even though they didn't need it."[24]

The same pattern seemed to prevail in most towns where the company did so much for its tenants. It cannot be stated that this was a characteristic developed alone by the paternalistic atmosphere of the company-owned community, but the attitude was enhanced by it and was one of the almost universal problems faced by town superintendents.

In summary, a general consideration of Western company towns will show that no one industry can be credited with developing typically "good" or "bad" communities. Paternalism in all its extremes existed throughout the West. Some companies controlled the entire life of the town, even attempting to tell their tenants how to vote. The company was the government, and some residents learned to expect almost everything from it, taking little initiative even in maintaining their own houses, while others demonstrated

23 *Ibid.*, supplement, 18.
24 Henry Jones interview.

126

considerable industry in their own behalf. Living in a company town was an advantage to those who took advantage of it, and even provided future financial security to some, while it was distinctly a disadvantage to others. Paternalism was a necessity, and hence an advantage, to the companies but one which most would gladly eliminate when all economic factors permitted such a move.

CHAPTER X

The Company Store

VIRTUALLY EVERY Western company town, at least before the 1940's, had its company store. Usually located near the center of population, the store served many functions. First and foremost, it was the community shopping center, where everything from vital workingmen's tools to nonessentials for the home might be purchased. Here a miner could buy his powder and fuses, a logger could buy his boots, and a housewife could purchase food, clothing, and lace curtains. Even automobiles sometimes could be obtained. Secondly, the company store frequently served as a town gathering place where gossip was exchanged, news was disseminated, and the men sat in front to talk about the same things they had discussed the day before. The company store often served also as pay office, post office, and bill-collection office, for it was in a unique position to take care of all such transactions for the community. Finally, it sometimes became a tool for company domination and control of the worker as employees found their very jobs at stake if they were to consider trading elsewhere. Whatever its function, the company store was once perhaps the most typical feature of the company town.

While most companies considered in this study were the owners of a single town, several firms had such extensive holdings that they were obliged to establish what might be termed a "chain" of towns. In such cases the company involved usually operated a chain of company stores also. Even one-town companies sometimes had their own form of chain store. In lumber companies, for instance, the store which operated in a mill town usually provided goods also for the company's logging camps. In a large camp a wide variety of goods was available in a permanent building. In small, temporary camps the store provided only the essentials. The McCloud Lumber Company operated a large logging camp called Pondosa. The company store was located in McCloud, but during the logging season three hundred to five hundred people lived in Pondosa and were provided with store services at the camp. When the season closed, of course, the camp was deserted.

General Operations

The administration of the company store was often handled by a special store department included within the regular company organization. In the case of larger organizations a subsidiary company was usually formed to handle all mercantile problems. In rare cases an outside firm would become recognized as the company store. At Camp Engle, Colorado, for example, the Tarabino brothers early established a general store and eventually came to function as the company store. Tarabino and Company cashed pay checks and did a scrip business amounting to six thousand dollars a month.[1]

The Colorado Supply Company is an example of a subsidiary corporation organized for mercantile purposes. Incorporated under Colorado law in August, 1888, this company served the various camps of the Colorado Fuel and Iron Corporation. Its first store opened in September, 1888, and by 1904 thirty-two stores were in operation. Gross sales in 1903 amounted to $2,694,368.68.[2] President of the Colorado Supply Company was J. C. Osgood, who was also chairman of the Board of Directors of Colorado Fuel and Iron. Included among the stockholders were officers and employees not only of Colorado Fuel and Iron, but also of the Rocky Mountain Coal and Iron Company and Victor-American Fuel Company.[3] This would indicate some effort on the part of Colorado

1 *Camp and Plant*, Vol. I (May 31, 1902), 460.
2 *Ibid.*, Vol. V (March 26, 1904), 242–44.
3 *Ibid.*, 244.

Supply to expand into areas other than those strictly controlled by Colorado Fuel and Iron, which, in fact, it did. Within C.F.&I. camps it operated strictly as a company store, with a virtual monopoly on all trade.

Phelps Dodge Mercantile Company is a subsidiary of Phelps Dodge Corporation. The history of this concern began in Bisbee in the 1880's. The leading general store in the mining camp was owned by a widow named Crossey and managed by a shrewd Irishman named Billy Brophy. James Douglas learned that employees of the Copper Queen were dissatisfied with the store and recommended that Phelps Dodge purchase it, retaining Brophy as manager. Through its broader contacts the company believed it could provide better and cheaper goods and, not incidentally, obtain a new source of revenue through the store.[4] The venture succeeded admirably and grew eventually into Phelps Dodge Mercantile Company. This organization established company stores in every town owned by Phelps Dodge thereafter, as well as other towns not owned by the company but where extensive Phelps Dodge operations were conducted.

In some cases the company department operating the store expanded its functions widely. At Trona, California, for example, the Mercantile Department of American Potash and Chemical Corporation handled a variety of company stores, such as the Trona Food Market, the Trona Drug Store, and the Trona Department Store. It also handled company scrip and the rebate system. This department was further responsible for operation of the Trona Club. The Trona Club included kitchen and dining facilities for private parties, a bowling alley, pool tables, a bar and cocktail lounge, and a card room. The Mercantile Department also maintained a regular pool hall, operated mainly for the single men, where sandwiches, doughnuts, rolls, and soft drinks were sold.

An extensive study of the company store in America was published in 1952 by Ole S. Johnson under the title, *The Industrial*

4 Cleland, *A History of Phelps Dodge*, 127.

Store.[5] Mr. Johnson's work applied to America as a whole, and most of his case studies were done in the East. Industrial stores, furthermore, included many company-owned stores not necessarily connected with company towns. His conclusions, however, seem generally to be valid as far as company stores in the West are concerned, and it is deemed advisable to discuss the company store in terms of some of his findings, illustrating with specific examples in the West, and noting any important exceptions.

With respect to the original need for company stores, Johnson came to the same conclusion frequently alluded to in this study—the fact that geographic isolation of the industries concerned influenced the establishment of these stores, but that the speeding up of all kinds of transportation and communication facilities has largely eliminated this condition today. It is this very economic change which has eliminated most of the company stores in the West, even though several company towns continue to exist.

Mr. Johnson pointed out that company stores had several advantages over any potential competitors in their respective areas. The fact that the store was located on company property near the mine or mill and had the exclusive privilege of collecting accounts through payroll deductions gave "the company store an unfair and monopolistic advantage over the independent store."[6] Whether or not the advantage was "unfair" may be conjectural, especially in the West, for in most cases the privilege of buying in the company store on credit was a luxury independent stores could not afford to give, and yet it was this luxury which attracted and held many workers. There is no evidence of any widespread protests on the part of independent merchants, and Johnson records only one such incident in his entire survey.

According to Johnson, much evidence exists to indicate that in earlier years workers were compelled to trade at the company store. The circumstance of living in an isolated region was nat-

5 Ole S. Johnson, *The Industrial Store.*
6 *Ibid.*, 90.

131

urally one contributing factor. In addition, both direct and indirect pressure was frequently used to enforce this trade. In recent years this practice has not prevailed.

Evidence from a few company towns in the West indicates that, in early years, compulsory trading in the company store was a condition of employment. At Sunnyside, Utah, for example, a number of stores and saloons existed away from the property of Utah Fuel Company. It is reported, however, that employees were expected to patronize the company store and that many men "lost their jobs for patronizing the other stores for things that could be obtained at much higher prices in the Company store."[7] In later years, the same resident reported, the company said nothing about trading with the stores below town if the men just bought a few things, but she considered this as simply "a cover-up for the company when a fuss was made about making the people trade with the company store." Company control extended so far that it had given a monopoly on the milk supply to the Big Spring Ranch, and it was highly difficult to obtain permission even to own a family cow.

The practice of compelling trade in the company store, however, seems not to have been as widespread as sometimes suggested. The Union Pacific Coal Company allowed a grocer from Laramie, Wyoming, to come to Hanna, solicit business and ship goods in on company trains. In the lumber-mill town of Caspar, California, the M. A. Nolan store gave effective competition to the company store. The manager of the company store once complained of this to the president of Caspar Lumber Company, who simply replied that he liked competition. It was healthy and, in his opinion, would not hurt the company.[8] It is interesting to note that freight was shipped into Caspar on company-owned boats, and this included the freight of the M. A. Nolan store.

Residents of many other towns report that, although the com-

7 Richins, "A Social History of Sunnyside," 3–4.

8 Interview with James W. Lilley, superintendent, Caspar Lumber Co., Caspar, Calif., April 13, 1962.

pany did not allow other stores to operate in town, employees were not afraid to purchase in stores of nearby communities. In Hilt, California, it was customary for at least one family to bring in a month's supply of food at a time from Ashland, Oregon, during winter months. The mother would have the groceries sent into town on the train, and apparently the company had no objections, even though a company store was operating.[9] A former company-store manager for Kennecott Copper Corporation declared:

> To my knowledge, through forty years service with Kennecott Copper Corporation, there never was any direct or indirect pressure used to compel workers to trade with the company store. It was certainly not a condition of employment.[10]

The relative price and quality of goods sold in company stores has been a matter of some controversy. With respect to quality, Johnson found that most company stores had the reputation of carrying only the top grades of meats and produce, as well as good quality merchandise in all other lines. Average prices, he found, were slightly higher in company stores. The most complete study of this type was made by the N.R.A., and it revealed average food prices in company stores to be from 2.1 per cent to 10.4 per cent higher than those of neighboring stores.[11]

Company stores in the West seemed generally to follow this pattern. Items purchased in the stores were generally of the highest quality, and company periodicals usually made it a point to mention the top-grade goods available. In the matter of pricing, it was generally true that the company store was higher. Several factors apparently contributed to this. First, since the company store often had no competition it could charge higher prices without losing sales. Secondly, costs to the company store were usually somewhat higher, because of the costs involved in shipping into isolated areas. Finally, the extension of credit by the company store was con-

9 Irene F. Tallis interview.
10 Letter from R. E. Andrews, Comptroller's Department, Kennecott Copper Corp., Chino Mines Division, Hurley, N.M., June 25, 1962.
11 Johnson, *Industrial Store*, 92.

sidered to warrant a slight increase in price, from the standpoint both of increased bookkeeping costs as well as convenience to the consumer.

In other cases, the company store was fully competitive with private merchants. Some towns, such as Caspar, California, would have competing stores right in town and would therefore have to meet their prices. In these situations the liberal extension of credit by company stores made slightly higher prices still feasible. The Phelps Dodge Mercantile Company is presently in competition with other concerns in every town where it operates. The general manager claims that Phelps Dodge prices are lower in many ways. On furniture, they do not take trade-ins, so their mark-up is not as great in the first place. No interest is charged for contract terms, which is a savings to those buying on credit. Phelps Dodge, said the manager, will not start a price war but will follow one in order to keep its prices competitive.[12]

The question of whether or not the company made unjust profits from company stores is controversial. Critics of the company-store system often charge that it was simply another way for the company to exploit the worker. It appears, however, that even though most companies did not lose anything through the operation of stores, such profits as accrued usually were not out of order. In many cases a rebate system operated in connection with the use of scrip, and employees would thus share in the profits. In Ajo, Arizona, Phelps Dodge still operates such a system. In other cases the profits were rather substantial. The Weed Lumber Company in California, for example, reported its net gain from the company store in 1911 to be $57,121.11.[13]

Scrip and Credit

The use of scrip was another controversial feature of the company store. Scrip was not universally used in the West, but where it

12 Interview with H. Lee Smith, general manager, Phelps Dodge Mercantile Co., Douglas, Ariz., March 13, 1962.
13 Weed Lumber Co., "Annual Report" (1911).

was used it served a variety of purposes. Primarily it was used as a method of credit, sometimes on the basis of money earned but not yet received, but frequently extended to future earnings. Scrip was a convenient bookkeeping method for companies which extended credit, for they did not have to keep track of individual items purchased, only of the total amount of scrip issued. Some companies also considered it a safety measure, for the total amount of cash necessary for the payroll was kept at a minimum. It has been charged that the extension of credit through scrip was used to keep workers in town by inducing them to remain forever in debt to the company store. Finally, the discounting of scrip by other merchants, and sometimes even by the company, for cash was an additional profit-making technique.

Johnson found that abuses of the scrip system were prevalent in all areas where it was used and that the practice of the company store of discounting its own scrip for cash was used by some companies for many years.[14] The evil of this practice lay in the fact that it resulted in an actual reduction in wages for those who could not wait until the end of the pay period for some cash, but this has been practically eliminated in recent decades. More common was the practice of non-company stores discounting company scrip in exchange for cash. The rate of the discount varied from 10 to 30 per cent. A long-time resident of Hanna, Wyoming, reported that when private liquor stores operated in town they would take company scrip, but at about 10 per cent discount.[15] It was not an unusual practice in other communities for someone who needed cash to sell his scrip to other persons at a discount. Even though the scrip was sometimes labeled as nontransferable, there seemed to be no practical way to control this practice.

The use of scrip was directly connected with the extension of credit, which had the effect, in some cases, of keeping the employee perpetually in debt to the company. The credit system, however,

14 Johnson, *Industrial Store*, 91.
15 Henry Jones interview.

had some advantages in that it served as a control on extravagance, and upon loan sharks, credit peddlers, and others who might exploit the somewhat helpless worker.[16] In defending the scrip system, Colorado Fuel and Iron Corporation published the following comment:

> Experience has shown, where the miner procures promiscuous credit from stores not connected with the mine, that quite regularly just before payday, some merchant being in doubt about the miner's pay being sufficient to cover all his debts, or about his willingness to settle, garnishees the Company for his wages, and by the time the debt and costs are all paid, the entire wages are consumed. At mines where there are no company stores these garnishments are numerous and a fruitful source of unnecessary expense to the miner.[17]

Some companies, especially Colorado Fuel and Iron, have been accused of intentionally keeping cash away from their employees. It might be observed, however, that the average resident of a company town needed very little cash so long as he could purchase all his needs on credit or with scrip. To counter such criticisms the president of Colorado Fuel and Iron issued the following statement in 1914:

> Colorado coal miners are paid twice per month. During the fiscal year preceding the strike the employees at the Colorado Fuel and Iron Company coal mines received 80.1 per cent. of their earnings in cash.
>
> Of the 19.1 per cent. of all earnings deducted by the company before making payment to the men, 11.73 per cent. represented purchases at our stores; 2.25 per cent. represented rent of houses; and the remaining 5.12 per cent. represented coal, board, hospital, powder and the customary charge of 50 cents per month for sharpening tools.[18]

[16] Johnson, *Industrial Store*, 91.
[17] *Camp and Plant*, Vol. V (March 26, 1904), 245, 247.
[18] *The Struggle in Colorado for Industrial Freedom*, Bulletin No. 15 (September 4, 1914), 2.

A long-time company clerk at Hanna, Wyoming, estimated that only 2 per cent of the employees here used up all their wages before they received them. Phelps Dodge Mercantile Company reports that today a few people still use up their entire pay check in deductions, but that the total number is insignificant. It seems apparent that those who could cry "I owe my soul to the company store" were relatively few in number, at least in the West.

A widespread practice in the West was the extension of credit through the company store for emergency relief, and most companies in the West have extended credit through times of depression. In many cases the company went so far as to extend credit even during a strike. In a recent Phelps Dodge strike, which lasted six months, the company store carried workers on credit for the entire period. A limit was placed on the amount of credit each man could have, depending upon the size of his family, but at the end of the strike approximately one million dollars in credit had accumulated. A special program was then set up for paying it off.

One might legitimately inquire into the motives of the company for extending such credit. "As a social or humanitarian measure," says Johnson, "it is indeed unique—to be able to draw groceries and other supplies from the retail store owned by the same company against which the workers are striking!"[19] A more practical consideration was obviously involved also. In the case of Phelps Dodge it was largely because the company wanted its men to stay, in order to have an available work force when the strike was settled. The company was certainly humanitarian in many ways, but motives of self-interest cannot be ignored.

The scrip used in company stores was by no means uniform in design. Most often it was composed of detachable coupons sold in books of various denominations from five to twenty dollars. Each book contained coupons ranging in value from one cent to one dollar. Sometimes metal tokens were used, and in other cases tokens were made of cardboard or other materials. They all served the

19 Johnson, *Industrial Store*, 91.

same purpose, however, of replacing cash in transactions between the employee and the company store.

Trona, California, provides a practical example of the operation of the scrip system. Scrip consisted of coupons sold in books of $5, $10, and $20 denominations. On a strictly voluntary basis an employee could take any portion of his pay in scrip, or he could receive scrip books as change when dealing with the company store. Users of scrip were required to purchase a full book at a time, and coupons would not be accepted by store clerks if they had been detached from the covers.

The company encouraged the use of scrip, and it could be spent anywhere in town, including the theater, pool hall, bar, and service station. From 1931 to 1957 the company also used tokens made of brass or aluminum. Since that time these tokens have become collector's items, with only two complete sets known to be in existence. Even the company does not now have such a set.[20]

Twice a year the company declared a rebate. At this time employees presented their empty scrip book covers, with their names written on them, and received their share of the profits according to the amount of scrip spent. The rebate was paid in cash. Certain inequities existed, however, for employees who lost their scrip book covers or moved out of town before turning them in were unable to participate in the dividend.

The significance of the company store in our present economy was examined by Mr. Johnson. The trend, he concluded, is toward a slight over-all reduction in the number of industrial stores in the United States, although the total volume of sales is on the increase. In the West, however, the company store located in the company town has almost totally disappeared. Companies which have owned towns for many years have now turned to leasing out their stores, as well as all other town business facilities, to other operators, even though the towns are still company owned. New company towns,

---

[20] For the story of Trona's interesting tokens, see Virginia Culver, "Tokens of Trona Bygone Epoch," *Coin World* (February 23, 1962).

such as Weed Heights, Nevada, are built with no intention of operating company stores, and the business sections are immediately leased. Only Phelps Dodge Corporation continues to operate a chain of company stores. Its gross sales are significant enough to have totaled $12,463,000 in 1961.[21] Individual company stores remain in only a few isolated towns. Except for the Phelps Dodge organization, the company store is no longer a significant institution in the West.

[21] Phelps Dodge Corp., *Annual Report* (1961).

CHAPTER XI

The End of the Company Town

T
HE STORY of the company town in Western America is, in
large measure, a reflection of the economic development of
the West. In the lumber industry, dozens of towns necessarily
sprang up as mills were established in the forests miles away from
other centers of population. In these areas lack of highways and
other transportation facilities made it essential for companies to
provide housing and other community needs. The growth of cities
and towns in the West, together with the development of modern
roads, highways, and automobiles, has largely eliminated this
necessity. In the coal fields, similar needs compelled the creation
of company towns, but the expansion of civilization, plus a decline
in the demand for coal, has eliminated them. Many towns erected
by copper companies at mines and smelters have been eliminated
or sold as it became desirable for workers either to commute from
nearby cities or to purchase their own homes in smelter communities. Other towns simply have been abandoned as ore has given
out. Economic necessity dictated the origin of the company town,
and economic considerations are largely responsible for its disappearance.

The switch away from company-town ownership sometimes
involves the unusual activity of "selling" an entire community. Of
particular interest in this movement is John W. Galbreath and
Company, a real-estate and land management firm of Columbus,
Ohio. Some companies, such as American Potash and Chemical
Corporation, have elected to sell their towns by themselves. Others
have turned the entire operation over to experienced real-estate

concerns. The Galbreath company has been America's most prominent broker of company towns.[1]

Galbreath has bought and sold company towns all over the country. The normal procedure is to purchase the entire community, including all houses, property, recreational facilities, and company-owned utilities. For the new owner, the town now becomes a money-making proposition. The Galbreath company must recover its investment and make a profit and to do so must convince long-time residents that they are going to benefit from the operation.

The first Western town to be purchased by Galbreath was the coal-mining town of Dragerton, Utah. Dragerton had been constructed during World War II by the federal Defense Plant Corporation and operated by the United States Steel Corporation. It was being sold by the War Surplus Administration. Galbreath took over in 1947, rehabilitated the townsite, and sold the homes to U.S. Steel employees. Henderson and Gabbs, Nevada, were also war surplus towns later handled by Galbreath. In 1955 the company took over all Kennecott's Western towns. Kennecott had originally decided to dispose only of its Utah villages but eventually saw the value of getting completely away from the problems of community ownership. Gerald H. Galbreath, Jr., made an offer on all real estate and, after it was accepted, simultaneously took over eight company towns in Arizona, New Mexico, Nevada, and Utah. Galbreath also handled the sale of Columbia, Utah, Climax, Colorado, and Clarkdale, Arizona, making at least fourteen Western towns sold since 1947.

Many unusual and challenging problems arise as Galbreath takes over a town. First, residents must be assured that all their interests will be protected. All kinds of questions immediately pour

[1] The following brief discussion is based largely on interviews with Gerald H. Galbreath, Jr., who handles the company's Western operations, and Harold Potter, who was project manager at Climax, McGill, and Kearny. The reader is also referred to Blank, "He Turned Company Towns into Home Towns," *American Business*, Vol. XXVIII, No. 9 (September, 1958).

into the company office. "What's going to happen to my house?" "How long before I have to decide whether or not to buy?" The company makes every effort to keep the interest of the people at heart and to set up an orderly, fair method of sale. Rules and regulations governing sales are posted, residents are given first choice on the houses they occupy, and F.H.A. loans usually are arranged. Community recreational councils are concerned with ball parks, which the company usually donates to the town. The company also becomes involved with community government, making suggestions concerning town councils, incorporation procedures, etc. Finally, it is recognized that 20 per cent of America's population is moving constantly. The company therefore must be prepared to take homes back and resell them. Galbreath still has offices at or near several of the Western towns it has sold.

To the credit of John W. Galbreath and Company, it can fairly be said that former company-town owners as well as residents are generally well pleased with the firm's activities.[2] Its reputation was well recognized in an editorial comment in a Leadville, Colorado, paper when the company established offices there in order to handle the sale and moving of Climax:

> Leadville welcomed a new, big business last week, and one that will be important locally for the next quarter of a century, according to present indications.
>
> The new business is the John W. Galbreath Company which has purchased the family housing units formerly owned and operated by the Climax Molybdenum Company.
>
> We know little of the Galbreath company other than what its employees themselves can tell us. However, from these reports and from other information we can obtain, we are impressed with the stature and integrity of this community and real estate-conscious operation.
>
> Climax was wise and fortunate in obtaining the Galbreath firm

2 This writer had personal interviews with Kennecott officials, including the manager of the Western Mining Division, as well as several employees in Hayden. All were highly pleased and well satisfied with Galbreath policies and procedures.

as purchaser of the "company" town. The new owners appear well-qualified to handle the many problems which are bound to arise and we feel certain that all who live in this area will benefit as a result of Galbreath's wisdom gained through experience in these matters.

The Galbreath company comes to the Leadville area with an impressive list of recommendations and other credentials. The Kennecott Copper corporation and United States Steel corporation are among the more impressive satisfied "customers" to be served by Galbreath. . . .

We honestly feel that, although Galbreath is primarily attempting to operate a successful business, the firm is nonetheless sincere in its attempt to "put families into their own homes in places they are proud to call 'home towns.' "[3]

It should not be assumed that the switch away from paternalism does not create problems for some communities and companies. Kennecott Copper Corporation, for example, ran into unexpected difficulty at Hayden, Arizona. After the community was sold to residents it incorporated itself, taking into its borders not only the residential area but also land where Kennecott's new smelter was going up. The Gila County Board of Supervisors had quietly approved these limits, suggested by the council, before the company realized how far they extended. Kennecott immediately asked the county attorney to act against the new independent community, charging that the petitioners had not been owners of real property and that, contrary to Arizona law, the incorporated area had included large uninhabitable areas. The county attorney held that the incorporation was legal, whereupon the company sought a writ of mandamus asking him to declare the town council illegal. In defense of the town's position J. Rodney Hastings, a young teacher elected mayor, declared that all towns have industrial areas and that taxes from Kennecott were necessary to provide street improvements, lights, garbage collection, and other services. "Kennecott unloaded the responsibility of the town," he charged,

3 *The Herald Democrat*, February 12, 1960.

"and now they don't want to support it."[4] The problem was finally settled by a compromise out of court, with Kennecott retaining the smelter land and a section of the tailings dump, but other property around the town was deeded to Hayden.[5]

In addition to the story of the big "change-over" from paternalism, it should be noted that a new kind of company town is beginning to spring up. The new company towns, such as San Manuel, Arizona, are well-planned, model communities. Development firms are hired to design and build the towns, homes are sold to workers, companies operate no local businesses, and shopping centers are leased or sold to local, independent merchants.

Finally, notice must be taken of the fact that, in some cases, new and unexpected use is being made of several one-time company towns which normally would have been abandoned. Tennant, California, has been donated to the Veterans of Foreign Wars and will probably be developed into a resort or haven as this organization sees fit.[6] Starkey, Oregon, has been donated to a youth organization and rehabilitated as a youth camp. The mining town of Holden, Washington, has been donated to the Lutheran Bible Institute and now serves as a summer retreat area for young adult groups sponsored by various Lutheran synods.[7] Ryderwood, Washington, was purchased in 1954 by an enterprising real-estate firm and converted into a haven for senior citizens. Within one year all homes had been sold and the new residents were actively building a dike and creating their own lake for boating, fishing, and swimming.[8] Since many company towns originally were located in ideal resort areas, there is no reason why new use cannot be made of them after their original purpose has been fulfilled.

[4] "Too Much Town; Kennecott Copper Corp. Balks at Incorporation of Hayden, Arizona," *Business Week* (April 16, 1957), 195.

[5] Interview with J. Rodney Hastings (first mayor of Hayden), Tucson, Ariz., March 22, 1962.

[6] Newspaper clippings with letter from T. H. Mutchler, public relations manager, International Paper Co., Long-Bell Division, Longview, Wash., May 21, 1962.

[7] *The Seattle Times*, October 18, 1960; and June 11, September 17, and January 27, 1961.

[8] *Ibid.*, April 8, 1954; June 2, 1955; and July 6, 1957.

144

In summary, the story of the company town as a feature of Western American development is a story with many facets. Created out of necessity, these towns grew in various ways. Some evolved from tent towns, mining camps, and other rugged frontier communities. Others were well planned from the beginning. Most were fully paternalistic, although the degree of company control varied widely. Company participation in recreational and community activities varied with need, location, and attitude of management, as was the case with respect to housing, sanitation facilities, and other community services. The gradual disappearance of the company town is a reflection of the general economic development of the West, with modern highways and automobiles making formerly remote areas no longer isolated. Most company towns have been eliminated, although many remain as communities of home owners still attached to the original industry. Others have been converted to attractive resorts, while still others have been completely abandoned.

Appendix

(Note: All the company towns identified by the writer in the course of his research are included in the following appendix. It should not be assumed that this is a complete list of all company towns which may have existed, for it is recognized that many could have been missed in each state. The purpose of the following list is to give only a short summary statement on each town which was found for the benefit of those who may be interested in particular states or industries.)

Arizona

Ajo (copper mine and smelter). Developed from an old-time mining camp which became the property of the New Cornelia Copper Company in the early part of this century. In 1931 Phelps Dodge Corporation took over. Ajo is still a Phelps Dodge company town, although a large private residential area exists outside company property. An attractive plaza and well-kept company homes make this a pleasant company town despite the desert heat.

Bagdad (copper mine and smelter). Bagdad is a company town of about 1,800 population, currently owned by the Bagdad Copper Corporation. It had its beginning about the turn of the century.

Bisbee (copper mining). Bisbee, which has evolved from a rugged mining camp of the nineteenth century, is not a full-fledged company town. Phelps Dodge owns all property, but most of the homes are privately owned, and most of the business is private. The town is incorporated and has its own government, independent of the company. Phelps Dodge Mercantile dominates the business of the community.

Christmas (copper mining). The town of Christmas grew slowly from a small mining camp established in the late nineteenth century. The post office was established in 1905. The camp has passed through the hands of several owners, including American Smelting and Refining Company, Christmas Copper Company, and Sam Knight Mining Lease, Inc. Sam Knight operated the property until it closed in 1950. At that time the town was abandoned.

Clarkdale (copper smelter). A model mining community, Clarkdale was laid out in 1914 by the United Verde Copper Company, whose ore came from the mines at Jerome. Clarkdale became the property of Phelps Dodge in the 1930's and was operated by them until 1953, when ore at Jerome gave out. The town was later sold, and though it is no longer a company-owned town, a cement plant is giving new life to the community.

Hayden (copper smelter). Hayden was built in 1911 as a smelter town for the Ray Consolidated Mining Company to process ore from the Ray mine. By 1933 Kennecott Copper had taken possession, and this company operated Hayden until 1955, when the town was sold to residents. Kennecott Copper still operates a smelter at Hayden, as does American Smelting and Refining Company. The latter company owns a few company houses at this location.

Helvetia (copper mining). Helvetia was an example of the old-time mining camp, existing from the 1890's until 1911. A company store existed, and the company participated in school activities, but Helvetia never became a full-fledged company town.

Inspiration (copper mining). Built in the 1920's, Inspiration is still a company town, although the company store and other paternalistic activities no longer exist. The Inspiration Consolidated Copper Company owned and operated the town as a residential area for key officials, supervisors, and skilled employees. Other workers lived in nearby Miami.

147

Litchfield Park (cotton plantation). This unique community was begun in 1917 when Goodyear Tire and Rubber Company began raising long-staple cotton in Arizona. It is still owned by Goodyear Farms and is one of the most attractive company towns in the West.

Marinette (cotton plantation). The Marinette Ranch was purchased by Goodyear in 1920. It was later sold to the J. G. Boswell Company and is the center of an 8,000-acre cotton tract. The settlement consists of a store, post office, and several labor camps, but it may not come fully into the category of a company town.

Morenci (copper mine and smelter). Morenci evolved from a late nineteenth-century mining camp. Phelps Dodge has built a completely new town since assuming control in the early part of this century. The oldest part of Morenci still reminds the visitor of a cliff-hung village, because houses are built rather haphazardly on the steep mountainsides. Two new developments, Stargo and Plantsite, are built on well-planned, terraced hillsides. Morenci is still a Phelps Dodge company town.

Ray (copper mining). This town grew slowly from a mining camp of the 1890's, and has passed through the hands of various owners. In 1955 the houses were sold by Kennecott Copper Corporation to the Galbreath company, who sold them to residents. The property remained in the hands of Kennecott, and all homes eventually will be moved to make way for the expanding mine.

San Manuel (copper mine and smelter). This new-type company town was built by Magma Copper Company in 1954. It was not to be a real company town, however, for the homes were built to be sold to residents, and the company operates no paternalistic enterprises.

Silver Bell (copper mine and mill). The present town and mill at Silver Bell were developed between 1951 and 1954 by the American Smelting and Refining Company. The town consists of 175 homes, 24 apartments, and a trailer court, all owned by the company. It was built just three miles from the old mining camp of Silver Bell, also operated by A. S. & R. until it closed in 1928.

Twin Buttes (copper mine). This mining camp was operated from about 1903 to 1926 but never became a fully developed company town.

Tubac (copper and other metals). Tubac was an abandoned Spanish presidio taken over by the Sonora Exploring and Mining Company in 1856. It had a short but colorful history as Charles D. Poston became practically a one-man ruler of the entire area. It was abandoned in the 1860's because of danger from Apache Indians.

California

Albion (lumber mill). Albion occupies a beautiful setting on the Mendocino coast and was the site of a lumber mill as early as the 1850's. The company-owned community developed about the turn of the century and was operated by various companies, beginning in 1891 with the Albion Lumber Company and ending in 1928 when the mill was owned by Southern Pacific. The mill stood idle until 1940, when it was dismantled and all buildings and machinery were sold. In 1949 the Masonite Corporation purchased most of the remaining Albion Lumber Company property. Little remains at Albion today to remind one of the once bustling mill town. Former company-owned houses which remain are all privately owned, and the former mill site is a resort area.

Bagdad-Chase (gold mining). Originally called Camp Rochester, the little mining camp of Bagdad-Chase was located in the Mojave Desert and owned by Bagdad-Chase Gold Mining Company. It flourished for approximately the first three decades of the twentieth century.

Cartago (mineral pumping and processing). This town was built in 1916 by the California Alkali Company. It continued to function, mainly as a bachelor's community, until the company went bankrupt in 1936. Cartago still exists as a small settlement at Owens Lake, but no longer as a company town.

Crannell (lumber mill). The Little River Redwood Company started operation of a sawmill at Crannell in 1909. The entire town was built and maintained by the company. It was an attractive community with about 135 well-painted houses, good roads, etc. In 1931 the company merged with Hammond Lumber Company, which then assumed control. Within a year the Crannell sawmill was shut down, and subsequently it was dismantled because the Hammond Lumber Company had other facilities on Humboldt Bay. In 1955 Georgia-Pacific Corporation bought the Hammond company and soon tore down most of the old homes at Crannell, although a few remain.

Davenport (cement plant). Davenport was built in 1906–1907 by the Coast Dairies and Land Company to house workers employed in the new Santa Cruz Portland Cement Company plant. The dairy company operated the town, including the store, for the benefit of the cement company, but as a money-making proposition. Homes were sold to residents in 1921.

Delleker (lumber mill). Delleker was once a mill town owned by Tarter, Webster & Johnson, a subsidiary of American Forest Products Corporation. The town was dismantled in 1954.

Eagle Mountain (iron mining). Eagle Mountain is wholly owned by the Kaiser Steel Corporation. The camp was first established in 1947 and has since been built to a town of about 300 homes. Located approximately sixty miles from the nearest town, it is an example of the continuing need, even in modern times, for company towns sometimes to be established.

Falk (lumber mill). The Elk River Mill and Lumber Company began operations about 1884. The mill was located in a valley, and the town thus grew all over the hills. The company operated a boardinghouse, cook house, and hotel and owned several homes. Operations were discontinued in 1937, and the town eventually was abandoned. Nothing remains today.

Feather Falls (lumber mill). Feather Falls was founded in 1938 by the Feather River Pine Mills Company. This company today is part of the Georgia-Pacific Corporation. It is still a company town with a population of about 500. Average house rental is about $30.00 a month. Not all employees live in the community.

Giant (explosives plant). Giant was a very small company town built only to house a few key personnel of the Giant Powder Company. It was typical of other tiny settlements built in order to keep key personnel close because of the transportation difficulties of early years. The plant was closed in 1960.

Glen Blair (lumber mill). Glen Blair was a small town which grew around a lumber mill established in the nineteenth century. It continued to operate under various companies until 1928, when the timber was depleted and the town was abandoned.

Graegle (lumber mill). Graegle was operated as a mill town by the Graegle Lumber Company until the 1950's. It was later purchased by a real-estate firm and is being developed into a recreational area.

Hammonton (gold dredging). This community was established in 1905 as headquarters of Yuba Consolidated Gold Fields. It was named for W. P. Hammon, founder of the company and a leader in the dredging industry. It was a pleasant town but has been completely abandoned for many years.

Hilt (or *Hilts*) (lumber mill). Although some settlement had long existed in the area of Hilt, the present town got its start about 1911–12. It is owned completely by the Fruit Growers Supply Company and has a population of approximately 500.

Ingot (copper mine and smelter). About 1922 the Afterthought Mining Company built a mine and smelter at Ingot. The small colony of company-owned houses was later abandoned after efforts to get copper from Copper Hill proved vain. Today the ruins of the abandoned mill still may be seen from the highway.

Johnsondale (lumber mill). Johnsondale was founded in 1936–37 by Mt. Whitney Lumber Company, now a division of American

151

Forest Products Corporation. It is still a fully-owned company town with a population of approximately 500.

Korbel (lumber mill). Settlement at Korbel, once called North Fork, was begun in the 1880's when the Korbel brothers began milling operations there. In 1913 the property passed into the hands of the Northern Redwood Lumber Company, and in 1956 Simpson Timber Company took over. Korbel was once a full-fledged company town of around one hundred homes, with company store, recreation hall, etc. Simpson has eliminated all services except a few company houses, and these gradually are being done away with.

McCloud (lumber mill). McCloud was founded in the 1890's by the McCloud River Lumber Company and was fully owned by the firm. The town consisted of about six hundred family dwellings as well as quarters for single men. The company store provided all needed goods for town residents. McCloud is a particularly attractive company community, with well-painted houses and attractive churches and schools. In 1963 all assets, including the town, were purchased by United States Plywood Corporation, and in 1965 this firm was making arrangements to transfer the town to non-company ownership.

Merced Falls (lumber mill). Merced Falls flourished in the 1920's and 1930's and was fully owned by the Yosemite Lumber Company. A town of mixed races, it consisted of about one hundred homes for white people and about fifty houses in a different section for Mexican and Negro workers. It is reported that Merced Falls was "more lively" than some company towns for it was fairly close to other communities. Also, it was ringed on three sides by private property where six saloons operated. Since the mill and town closed down every building has been removed.

Metropolitan (lumber mill). This small town began with the establishment of a mill by the Metropolitan Lumber Company about 1905. The company closed its operations here about 1923, and all the houses eventually were moved.

Navarro (lumber mill). Formerly called Wendling, the tiny mill town of Navarro was begun in 1903 when the Wendling Mill and Lumber Company built a sawmill. In 1905 it was purchased by the Stearns Lumber Company, and in 1913 the Navarro Lumber Company took over. The mill was purchased by the Albion Lumber Company in 1920 and ceased operations in 1927. Today nothing remains of the original mill and settlement.

Navarro-by-the-Sea (lumber mill). This was another tiny settlement of only about fifteen houses. The mill was operated by the Navarro Lumber Company in the latter nineteenth century, closing in 1890. Today the area is an oceanside resort.

New Cuyama (oil fields). New Cuyama is not a company town according to the definition set up in this work. It is included here, however, as an example of the modern trend in company community building. It was built in 1950 by the Richfield Oil Corporation with the express intent of selling homes to town residents. Its government comes under the county Board of Supervisors.

Newburg (lumber mill). Newburg was a small company town supporting the mill of the Eel River Valley Lumber Company from the 1880's until the 1930's. The settlement was abandoned when the mill closed during the depression.

Rockport (lumber mill). Lumber mill operations existed at Rockport as early as the 1880's, and a camp gradually arose in that area. Early employees were mostly single men and lived in cabins. The first modern family dwellings were built in 1925 by the Finkbine-Guild Lumber Company. The Rockport Redwood Company took over in 1938. The sawmill was shut down in 1957, when the town had a population of about 500. Rockport was once a full-fledged company town, but now only a few houses are maintained for the benefit of the small number of men needed to manage the company's tree farm.

Samoa (lumber mill). Located on a peninsula in Humboldt Bay, the town of Samoa was established by the Vance Lumber Company, which built a mill there in the 1890's. In 1901 the property was taken over by the Hammond Lumber Company, which operated a pleasant, fully paternalistic company town. Georgia-Pacific acquired the Hammond Company in 1956 and since then has eliminated the company store. Homes are still company owned and maintained. The bungalow type homes and well-kept yards make Samoa one of the more attractive company towns.

Scotia (lumber mill). One of the best-known company towns in California, Scotia is still owned completely by the Pacific Lumber Company. Here are located the company's huge redwood mill and lumber manufacturing plant. Sawmill operations began in the 1880's, and the settlement was first called Forestville, the name being changed in 1888. The Pacific Lumber Company once owned every business enterprise in town, including a store, theater, bank, hospital, butcher shop, and hotel. Today only the hotel is operated by the company, with other businesses leased to private firms. The old bank building now houses a most interesting museum.

Standard (lumber mill). Standard is entirely owned by Pickering Lumber Corporation. It was begun about 1910 by the Standard Lumber Company, which sold out to Pickering in 1920.

Stirling City (lumber mill). Stirling City was not a fully-owned company town, but is mentioned as one of those towns in which a particular company had a substantial interest. For many years after about 1930 Diamond National Corporation owned a substantial number of the homes in the town as well as some commercial establishments. Diamond's section of Stirling City could be considered a modified version of the company town.

Tennant (logging town). Most logging camps were temporary camps used only during the logging season and then not providing many family residences. Tennant, however, is one of the few logging headquarters which became permanent towns. It was built in 1921 by the Weed Lumber Company, which was later acquired by Long-Bell Lumber Company. In 1950 it was donated to the Veterans of Foreign Wars.

Trona (mineral pumping and processing). From the early

1900's until 1953 the town of Trona was fully owned and controlled by American Potash and Chemical Corporation and its predecessors. The company still operates a large plant at this Searles Lake site where borax and other mineral products are produced. In 1953 the company decided to sell the town. All homes are now privately owned and all businesses are operated by private concerns. Trona is a thriving, independently governed community but still depends solely upon the company operations for its continued existence.

Weed (lumber mill). The town of Weed grew around a lumber mill established by the Weed Lumber Company in the 1890's. The company later merged with the Long-Bell Lumber Company, which operated the mill and town until its merger with International Paper Company in 1956. International Paper immediately got out of the company-town business by selling all homes except a few maintained for top management officials. During all of Weed's history not all employees lived in the company town, for a residential and business area existed outside company property. Weed was therefore an unusual combination type community.

Westend (mineral plant). Westend was founded in 1919 by the West End Chemical Company, now a division of Stauffer Chemical Company. It is the location of a plant for pumping brines from beneath the dry bed of Searles Lake for producing potash, borax, and other chemicals. No business facilities existed in Westend, most employees going to nearby Trona to shop. The town is currently in the process of dissolution.

Westwood (lumber mill). Westwood, in Lassen County, was established in 1913 by the Red River Lumber Company and later taken over by Fruit Growers Supply Company. It has been said that its huge mill, which was the center of lumbering in a fifty-mile radius, was once the largest lumber mill in the world. In 1955 the town was purchased by a Los Angeles real-estate firm. It has since been converted into a community of senior citizens.

Colorado

(Note: Colorado Fuel and Iron Corporation owned several coal-mining camps in the latter part of the nineteenth century and the early decades of this century. It has been difficult to determine where all of these camps were, even in correspondence with the company. The camps listed below as belonging to Colorado Fuel and Iron were compiled from *Camp and Plant*, a company publication, for the years 1901 and 1902. Some of the camps, such as Walsen, were actually part of larger non-company-owned communities, but the company still owned many homes, a company store, recreation hall, etc. on company property adjacent to the town. They are listed here because the company continually listed and considered them as company camps. It is not assumed that the camps listed as belonging to C. F. & I. form a complete list of this firm's towns, but it will serve at least to indicate the extent of this company's operations in southern Colorado.)

Anthracite (coal mining). This was a small C. F. & I. camp in Gunnison County. In 1901 the mine employed fifty-four men, and the camp had a store, small public school, and a small circulating library.

Baldwin (coal mining). This was a coal-mining camp once owned by the Rocky Mountain Fuel Company.

Berwind (coal mining). This C. F. & I. camp in Los Animas County supported a mine where, in 1901, 398 men were employed.

Boettcher (cement plant). This community was founded in 1926 by the Ideal Cement Company, which still owns the townsite. It was named after the company president, Charles Boettcher.

Brookside (coal mining). At this camp of seven hundred people, Colorado Fuel and Iron Company owned only ten homes in 1902. The company dominated the town, however, with its sociological department providing many activities and with a company store in operation.

Cardiff (coal mining). At this C. F. & I. camp sixty-six men were employed in 1901.

156

Climax (molybdenum mining). Founded in the late 1920's, Climax was the company-owned town of the Climax Molybdenum Company. The mine at Climax is the largest molybdenum mine in the world. Everything in the town was company owned. At an elevation of 11,320 feet, Climax was reputed to have had the highest post office in the United States. Undoubtedly it was the highest company town. In 1960 the town was sold to John W. Galbreath and Company. Homes were then sold to employees and moved to Westpark, a housing development near Leadville. Climax is now virtually abandoned.

Coal Creek (coal mining). This C. F. & I. camp in Fremont County employed 177 men in 1902.

Coalbasin (coal mining). This camp housed 269 miners for C. F. & I. in 1902.

Cokedale (coal mining). This coal-mining community was owned by the American Smelter and Refining Company. In 1940 it had a population of 500. Coke from ovens at Cokedale was shipped to the smelter at Leadville.

Crested Butte (coal mining). Originally a gold camp of the 1880's, Crested Butte eventually became a camp of C. F. & I. The camp had, in 1902, a three-room school, a drugstore, and a surgeon who also served Anthracite. The mine here employed 370 men.

Delagua (coal mining). This Los Animas County camp was established in 1903 by the Victor-American Fuel Company.

Delcarbon (coal mining). In 1940 this town of 300 population was owned jointly by the Calumet Fuel Company and Utah Fuel Company. It had once been called Turner, having been opened by a company by the same name.

El Moro (coal mining). This Colorado Fuel and Iron camp supported a mine employing 125 men in 1901.

Engleville, or *Camp Engle* (coal mining). This C. F. & I. camp illustrated the profuse mixing of nationalities which existed in the coal fields. In 1902 the mine here employed 140 Italians, 94 Mexicans, 64 Slavs, 60 English, and 12 native-born Americans.

157

Gulch Mines (coal mining). In 1901 the two Gulch mines employed 138 men. The C. F. & I. camp here had a company store, a one-room school, a fifty-volume library, and a surgeon who also served other areas.

Hastings (coal mining). This village was established by the Victor-American Fuel Company in 1893. An explosion in 1923 closed the mine.

Herzon (coal mining). The mine at Herzon, located in Huerfano County, employed 173 men in 1902. In that year a new company store was being erected as well as many new company houses, as plans were being laid to make Herzon one of the largest coal camps of Colorado.

Louviers (explosives manufacturing). Louviers was founded in 1906–1907 by E. I. Du Pont de Nemours & Company. It was the site of a plant for the manufacture of high explosives. It was a part of a chain of company towns owned by Du Pont. In 1961 homes were sold to employees.

Morley (coal mining). The Colorado Fuel and Iron town was settled in 1875. It became a model camp of 600 population. Its neat concrete houses were surrounded by attractive gardens, and it was apparently one of the better C. F. & I. towns. The town ceased to exist in 1956 when the Morley mine closed. It was one of the last company towns of C. F. & I.

Mt. Harris (coal mining). Founded in 1914, this town was apparently owned jointly by the Harris Coal Company and the Colorado-Utah Coal Company. The Harris company was dominant, and A. B. Harris was the first manager of the town. The buildings belonging to one coal company were painted gray, and those of its rival a bright yellow. The Harris company owned a store, boardinghouse, and many recreational facilities. It is reported to have been an outstanding coal company town. The town ceased to exist in 1955 and no buildings remain on the property at the present time.

Orient (coal mining). The Colorado Fuel and Iron camp was opened in 1882. In 1902 the mine employed 122 men. It was located in Saguache County.

Pictou (coal mining). This C. F. & I. camp, located in Huerfano County, was founded in 1887. In 1902 the mine employed 122 men. The town consisted of about seventy dwellings plus boarding-houses for both white and colored workers. It also had a company store.

Primero (coal mining). In 1902 the C. F. & I. mine at Primero employed 420 men, and the company town boasted a population of 2,000. In that year a large number of additional model cottages were being erected. Primero was a large mine, producing more than 68,000 tons of coal a month. The town was abandoned in 1925, and since then all buildings have been torn down. It was located in Los Animas County.

Redstone (coal mining). This C. F. & I. town was located in Pitkin County and was founded around 1900 by J. C. Osgood, an official of the company. It was one of C. F. & I.'s better towns, built as a model village. In 1902 the mine employed ninety-five men. The town had a company store, reading room, clubhouse, and a library of 422 books. Contrary to the pattern in most company towns, the cottages at Redstone were painted different colors, thus making the town more attractive. With the decline of mining the workers moved away, and the houses eventually were sold as summer residences.

Robinson (coal mining). Located near Walsenburg, Robinson was a camp belonging to C. F. & I. Employed at the mine were 109 men.

Rockvale (coal mining). Rockvale was a C. F. & I. camp in Fremont County. The town had a company store, school, and a surgeon. The mine employed 394 men in 1902.

Rouse (coal mining). This C. F. & I. camp consisted of about 125 homes in 1902, over half of which were owned by the miners themselves. There was also a company boardinghouse with accommodations for fifty men.

Segundo (coal mining). Segundo and Primero were both new C. F. & I. camps in 1902. In that year many more model dwellings were being erected to shelter the men employed at the coke ovens at Segundo and the mines at Primero. A single school district served both towns, as did a single company surgeon. Employed at Segundo were 799 men. The homes were built of red clay brick and the window frames and doorways were painted a bright blue.

Somerset (coal mining). Mining at Somerset was begun in 1905 by Utah Fuel Company. The property was purchased by U.S. Steel in 1950, and in 1960 the houses were sold to individuals.

Sopris (coal mining). Sopris was one of Colorado Fuel and Iron's oldest coal camps. The town originally had been established in the 1870's by E. R. Sopris, but C. F. & I.'s first mine was opened in 1887. The mine and coke ovens at Sopris employed 318 men in 1902. The mine was once the largest producer in Los Animas County.

Starkville (coal mining). Starkville was a C. F. & I. camp established in the 1890's. In 1902 over six hundred men were employed in the mine and coke ovens here.

Tercio (coal mining). Although a few settlers had previously inhabited the area, Tercio became a C. F. & I. camp in 1901. Tents and shacks typified the first settlement, but within one year the company had built one hundred cottages for employees, and the tents and shacks were disappearing.

Tobasco (coal mining). In 1902 the Tobasco mines and coke ovens employed 485 men. The settlement was a C. F. & I. camp.

Valdez (coal mining). Valdez was the camp supporting the Frederick Mine, one of the largest coal mines in southern Colorado. The town was dismantled in 1961.

Walsen (coal mining). Many C. F. & I. workers owned their own homes at Walsenburg, but the company also owned several houses at its camp here. In 1902 about three hundred men were employed in the two Walsenburg mines, representing thirteen different nationalities. The company had a store at the camp and provided recreational facilities for employees.

Wootton (coal mining). In 1911 the settlement of Wootton was completely owned and managed by the Wootton Land and Fuel Company. It was practically a little city-state, for whatever was needed was produced from surrounding lands. Company farms produced meat, milk and vegetables for the three hundred employees and their families. Company houses, which varied from four to eight rooms in size, were comfortable and sometimes even ornate.

Idaho

Cobalt (cobalt mining). Cobalt was so named in 1944 when the Calera Mining Company purchased the property of the Blackbird Mine. The town, originally called Forney, was not always a company town. Calera owned about 90 per cent of the houses at Cobalt during its mining operations there. The mines closed in 1958 after the company was unable to renew its contract for cobalt ores with the federal government, which financed the opening of cobalt mines in Cuba instead. The town of Cobalt was abandoned.

Conda (phosphate mine). Conda, a small model village, was erected in the 1920's by Anaconda Copper Mining Company. The company store was operated on a profit-sharing basis, and the community generally maintained a good spirit of co-operation. In 1950 the town was sold to the J. R. Simplot Company, which continues to mine phosphate and operate the company housing.

Headquarters (logging camp). Headquarters was founded in 1928 as a logging camp and later became a supply and equipment headquarters for all logging camps of Potlatch Forests, Inc. Here the company owns about ninety homes and provides a community hall as well as many other recreational facilities. Originally the company provided a school and a teacher for the first six grades, but today the local school district pays the teacher while the company still provides the school building.

Patterson (tungsten mining). Now a ghost town, Patterson was once a thriving company town where over three hundred men were employed in the mines. The Bradley Mining Company, who took over the mines in 1938, owned the houses, store, and all utilities.

Potlatch (lumber mill). Potlatch was founded in 1906 by Potlatch Lumber Company, which later merged with two other firms to form Potlatch Forests, Inc. The company owned the entire townsite, including 270 homes, a store, hotel, garage, and bank. The garage and bank were later sold to private firms. The company also provided adequate recreational facilities. In 1952 the company offered its homes for sale to employees, believing that home ownership would make for better employee-employer relationships. The town was incorporated in that year.

Stibnite (mining for gold and other metals). The Yellow Pine Mine at Stibnite operated from 1932 to 1952. It was the property of the Bradley Mining Company. After 1952 all facilities (including mining, milling, and smelting plants as well as all housing) was sold for removal from the premises.

Montana

Bonner (lumber mill). Bonner was founded in the 1880's by the Blackfoot Milling Company. (This company, incidentally, was formed by A. B. Hammond and his brother, who later formed the Hammond Lumber Company which owned some company towns in California.) The mill and townsite, purchased in 1910 by the Anaconda Company, are still operated by this firm's lumber department. It is a community of approximately 1,000 population and is said to be one of the outstanding sawmill towns in the United States. Its well-kept homes, paved streets, and fine landscaping all contribute to making Bonner an attractive community.

Colstrip (coal mining). Colstrip was founded in 1923–24 by the Northern Pacific Railroad Company, which owned the town until 1959. The mine and town were operated for the railroad by Foley Brothers, Inc., of St. Paul, Minnesota. In 1959 the town was purchased by the Montana Power Company. Colstrip was once a large community, but today only about thirty company houses are rented, owing to the decline in coal business. Residents are looking forward to the time when Montana Power will begin to use coal as their generating fuel. The Colstrip mine is particularly interesting for it is one of the largest open-pit, or strip, coal mines in the country.

Somers (lumber mill). The mill and settlement at Somers were established in 1901 by the John O'Brien Lumber Company, sponsored by the Great Northern Railroad. In 1907 Great Northern bought out John O'Brien and changed the name to Somers Lumber Company. Houses were all owned by the company and rented for $5.00 to $10.00 a month. In 1948 the town was sold to the Alex Shulman Company, of Seattle, and it is no longer a company town.

Warland (lumber mill). Warland was founded around 1929 by the Baird-Harper Lumber Company to support the establishment of a sawmill. It was a small town, with a peak population of about 300. Few recreational facilities were provided by the company, for Warland was located in an area with ample opportunity for fishing, hunting, and other outdoor sports. The mill ceased operating in 1926, and many of the homes were sold and moved to other locations, mostly by small ranchers in the area.

Nevada

Gabbs (magnesium mining). This community of about 125 houses was built during World War II by the Defense Plant Corporation. It supplied ore for the magnesium plant at Henderson. After the war two Ohio companies, the Standard Slag Company and Basic, Inc., purchased the mine and town. Later John W. Galbreath and Company purchased the townsite and sold the homes to individuals.

163

Henderson (magnesium plant). Henderson was constructed during World War II by the Defense Plant Corporation to provide housing for employees of Basic Magnesium, Inc. Although the government built the town, the company provided the housing administration and such government as existed. After the war the town was purchased by John W. Galbreath and Company, who sold the houses to individuals. It is now an incorporated community.

McGill (copper smelter). McGill was brought into existence about 1908 by the Nevada Consolidated Copper Company, which operated the largest smelter in the state. In later years Nevada Consolidated was taken over by Kennecott Copper Corporation. McGill reached a population of around 3,000. In 1955 the town was sold, like other Kennecott towns, to residents of the community.

Ruth (copper mining). Ruth, too, was founded by Nevada Consolidated about 1908 and eventually became one of Nevada's important copper mines. Housing was sold to the Galbreath company by Kennecott in 1955, but the land remains with Kennecott because of the possibility of mine expansion.

Weed Heights (copper mine and concentrator). Weed Heights is a modern, attractive company town owned by the Anaconda Company. It was built in 1951 and 1952 as part of a $40,000,000 investment by the company in the development of the Yerrington mine. Here an 87 per cent pure copper precipitate is produced which is shipped to the smelter at Anaconda, Montana, for refining. Weed Heights is said to be one of the most well-constructed and attractive mining camps in the country.

New Mexico

Catalpa (coal mining). This was a camp of the Colorado Fuel and Iron Corporation. In 1902 the mine employed about 226 men. It was located in McKinley County.

Dawson (coal mining). In 1905 Phelps Dodge acquired extensive coal-mining properties at Dawson. Coal was needed for the

164

support of railroads built and operated by the company. A large company-owned community was created, and former residents have expressed complete satisfaction with company control of the town. A large Phelps Dodge Mercantile store existed which served not only Dawson but also surrounding farming areas. When Dawson closed in the 1940's, many employees were transferred to other Phelps Dodge towns. The town was completely dismantled, and nothing remains of it today.

Gamerco (coal mining). Gamerco was a large coal-mining camp built by the Gallup American Coal Company in 1921. It was a well-planned community designed and constructed by an engineering firm hired by the company. At its peak it had a population of about 1,500. Gamerco ceased to be a company town in 1945 when it was purchased by a group of businessmen from Gallup.

Gibson (coal mining). This C. F. & I. camp housed employees working at both the Gallup and Weaver mines. In 1902, 187 men were employed at Gallup and 233 at Weaver. Company housing extended in practically a continuous line between the two mines. When the Weaver mine opened, the company built sixty-five new four- and six-room model houses.

Hurley (copper smelter). Hurley began in 1910 when the Chino Copper Company built a mill to process ore mined at Santa Rita. The two company towns were connected by railroad. It later became the property of the Kennecott Copper Corporation. At its peak, Hurley boasted a population of over 2,000. In 1955 it was sold along with other Kennecott towns, and the following year it became an incorporated community.

Madrid (coal mining). Mining activity in the vicinity of Madrid goes back to the 1880's and the 1890's when the government as well as private individuals operated a number of small mines in the area. The town of Madrid grew gradually in the nineteenth century as coal mining increased. The property early was operated by the Santa Fe Railroad. When Santa Fe decided to quit its coal

165

operations, the property was leased to Colorado Fuel and Iron, who operated it for four or five years then abandoned it. Shortly thereafter Mr. G. A. Kaseman, an Albuquerque coal dealer, took over and operated it as the Albuquerque and Cerrillos Coal Company. Under this company the town rapidly grew and became one of the well-known company towns of the West. It was a better-than-average coal town, as indicated by the fact that employees owning their own homes in nearby Cerrillos preferred to live in Madrid and pay rent because Madrid early had the conveniences of electricity and water in the homes. The annual Christmas celebration was a most colorful affair which received wide publicity. Today the property is still owned by the Albuquerque and Cerrillos Coal Company, but the town is virtually abandoned as the market for coal has been lost.

Santa Rita (copper mining). Sporadic copper mining had been done at Santa Rita throughout the nineteenth century. In 1909, however, it got its start as a modern mine with the opening of a successful open-pit mine by the Chino Copper Company. A company-owned town which grew up around the mine included a company store, hospital, school, social hall, and theater. Santa Rita eventually became part of Kennecott Copper Corporation. In 1955 the homes, but not the property, were sold, along with the sale of all Kennecott's towns. The houses will be moved as the mine expands.

Tyrone (copper mining). Tyrone was a copper-mining town built by Phelps Dodge in 1916–17 at a cost of one million dollars. It was a well-designed, model mining camp intended to support the company's Burrow Mountain mine. The mine, however, was never a large producer, and the town was abandoned in 1921.

Waldo (coal mining). Waldo was a small coal-mining camp in the Madrid area, established around the turn of the century by the Santa Fe Railroad. Colorado Fuel and Iron also operated there for a few years. In 1902 C. F. & I. employed twenty-nine men.

Oregon

Algoma (lumber mill). Algoma, in Klamath County, was once a community owned by the Algoma Lumber Company.

Brookings (lumber mill). Brookings, established sometime before 1920, was originally owned by the California-Oregon Lumber Company. By 1925 internal difficulties in the company caused it to liquidate its holdings, and the town was sold to private residents.

Dee (lumber mill). For many years Dee was owned by the Oregon Lumber Company. It was sold in 1958 to Hines Lumber Company, which liquidated the community. All houses have been removed.

Gilchrist (lumber mill). Gilchrist was established in 1938 by the Gilchrist Timber Company and is still a company town.

Grand Ronde (logging camp). Grand Ronde was a logging headquarters for the Long-Bell Lumber Company. It had about 150 company houses and a company store. These were sold in the 1950's.

Kinzua (lumber mill). Kinzua was founded in 1927 by the E. D. Wetmore family to provide housing for employees of their lumber mill. It is still completely owned by the Kinzua Corporation and has a population of about 800. Not all employees live in town, for some now commute from towns twelve to twenty-five miles away. Recreational facilities include two company-owned lakes which are kept stocked by the company with rainbow trout.

Pondosa (lumber mill). The mill at Pondosa was built in 1925–26 by the Stoddard Lumber Company. The post office was established in 1927. The town passed through the hands of the Collins Pine Company to the Mt. Emily Lumber Company, a subsidiary of Valsetz Lumber Company. In 1953 the town's fifty-three homes, eleven industrial buildings, general store, and hotel were sold at auction for a total of $33,925.

Powers (logging headquarters). Powers was established in 1915 as a logging headquarters for the Smith-Powers Logging Company. It did not remain as a company town for many years, how-ever, as the company-built homes were quickly sold to employees. Powers eventually grew into a large, active lumbering community.

Shevlin (logging headquarters). Shevlin was interesting be-cause it was typical of the many mobile logging camps which once existed. Belonging to the Shevlin-Hixon Company, it was moved several times in the Klamath and Deschutes County area. The post office was discontinued in 1951.

Starkey (logging headquarters). For many years Starkey was a logging headquarters for the Mt. Emily Lumber Company. It eventually was purchased by Valsetz Lumber Company and was liquidated by 1955.

Valsetz (lumber mill). Valsetz is still a fully owned company town of the Valsetz Lumber Company, which now is a division of the Boise Cascade Corporation. It was purchased in 1946 from the Cobbs-Mitchell Lumber Company. It had been constructed prior to World War I. Valsetz is one of the few remaining com-pletely isolated lumber-mill towns. It will undoubtedly remain a company town until such time as the mill closes.

Vaughn (lumber mill). This town was established in the 1920's by Snellstrom Brothers Lumber Company. It was purchased by Long-Bell in 1944 and is now owned by International Paper. It is a combination mill and logging town.

Wauna (lumber mill). Wauna was established in 1912 and is still owned by the Wauna Lumber Company. It is beautifully located on a 1,030-acre tract with more than two miles of water front on the Columbia River. Peak population was about 300. About 1960 the lumber mill closed down, and in 1962 it was still in the process of liquidation. No change yet had been made in the town except that lumber manufacturing had been discontinued.

Wendling (lumber mill). This Booth-Kelly Lumber Company town was built to support a mill established in 1898. The mill closed in 1945, and the town was liquidated.

Westfir (lumber mill). The mill at Westfir was established about

168

1925 by Colonel Kelly of the Booth-Kelly Lumber Company. Its original purpose was to produce ties and lumber for the Southern Pacific Railroad. The town grew from an original tent colony surrounding the mill. In later years, the property was owned by Western Lumber Company and, finally, by Edward Hines Lumber Company. It is still owned by Hines, although homes are now being sold to workers.

Wilark (logging operation). Wilark was the center of logging operations for the Wilson and Clark Lumber Company, from which the town took its name. It consisted of over three hundred men, mostly single, living in bunkhouses. It had a commissary, post office, cook house, machine shop, and a few small family houses. About 1929 the town was moved as the company bought into another operation. In 1944 the company liquidated, and Wilark ceased to exist.

Utah

Bacchus (explosives plant). Bacchus was built in 1913 to house key personnel employed at the new Hercules Powder Company plant near Salt Lake City. It was an attractive, well-kept village of forty-one homes. Beginning in 1941, most of the homes were removed from the premises, and the company today maintains only six houses at that site. The plant, however, has expanded to become a major explosives and missile center.

Castle Gate (coal mining). Castle Gate was an early mining community, dating from about 1883. It passed through the hands of several coal companies but eventually came under the ownership of the Utah Fuel Company. In 1960 this company sold all company housing. Castle Gate has been an incorporated community since 1914.

Clear Creek (coal mining). Clear Creek, located six miles south of Scofield, was founded about 1898 by the Utah Fuel Company. Like many other early communities, it was a tent village until better housing could be built by the company. The company owned

169

everything in town and rented houses for about $12.50 a month. In 1952 the town was sold to the Independent Coal and Coke Company.

Columbia (coal mining). Columbia was constructed about 1922 by Columbia Steel Company, a subsidiary of U.S. Steel Corporation. The mine was operated for the purpose of supplying coking coal to the company plant at Ironton. By 1923 the community had grown to a population of about 650. The townsite consisted of modern company-owned houses, bunkhouses for single men, a company store, boardinghouses, confectionary, amusement hall, and barbershop. About 1947 the entire town was purchased by John W. Galbreath and Company and homes were sold to individuals.

Consumers (coal mining). Located in Carbon County, Consumers was the residence of employees of Consumers Mutual Coal Company in the 1920's and 1930's.

Copperton (copper mining). Copperton was built in the 1920's by Utah Copper Company to house employees from the famous open-pit mine at Bingham. Since the community was located on the main tourist route to Bingham, the company made a show place of Copperton by using copper wherever possible in the construction of the homes. Copperton was strictly a residential community, with residents going to Bingham or other nearby communities to shop. Utah Copper was eventually absorbed by Kennecott Copper Corporation. In 1955 Copperton ceased to be a company town as houses were sold, along with those of all Kennecott towns, to individuals.

Dividend (lead, silver, gold, and copper mining). Located in Utah County about five miles east of Eureka, Dividend was a model mining community built by Tintic Standard Mining Company. It had a modern store, ice plant, hospital, ample recreational facilities, and, from 1924 to 1925, its own newspaper. It had homes for 100 families and hotel accomodations for 375 single men. By

1951 only a few buildings and a watchman remained at the location.

Dragerton (coal mining). Dragerton was constructed by the Defense Plant Corporation during World War II. The town was built to house coal miners employed at the Horse Canyon mine and consisted of 721 homes. It was operated by U.S. Steel and therefore is included here as a company town, although actually it was a government town. In 1947 the town was purchased by John W. Galbreath and Company and sold to residents.

Garfield (copper smelter). Garfield was founded in 1905 as a joint effort of Utah Copper Company and American Smelting and Refining Corporation. The latter had a one-third interest in the smelter and community. The town was built to house workers for the new smelter which took its ore from the Bingham mine. The town included 394 company-owned houses and became the property of Kennecott Copper Corporation when this firm took over the interests of Utah Copper. In 1955 the town was sold, along with all other Kennecott towns in the West. Homes were sold for removal as the smelter at Garfield was eliminated. Today nothing remains of this former smelter town.

Grass Creek (coal mining). Grass Creek is particularly significant here because it was operated by the dominant church in Utah, the Church of Jesus Christ of Latter-day Saints. Grass Creek was settled in 1883 when a number of Mormons went to work in the adjacent mines. The Union Pacific Railroad then owned the mines and houses but closed the mines, tore down the houses, and abandoned the camp in 1886 and 1887. A church-owned combination meeting and school house was left standing and in 1901 was moved to the new location. In the 1890's the church began developing its own mine in the Grass Creek area, and several church members moved there to work. The church-owned Grass Creek Coal Company did not own all housing, for many men began to build their own homes at the mine. The company journal shows, however, that Grass Creek had all the elements of a company town. The company owned homes, collected rent, sold coal to employees, and provided supplies from the company store. Church tithing orders were accepted at the mine store in lieu of cash. That this town operated like most early company towns is seen in the fact that the company deducted for rent, board, coal, and other things from the miner's wages.

Hiawatha (coal mining). Hiawatha was a company-owned community of the United States Fuel Company. It was an unusually attractive mining town, with trees, lawns, flower gardens, and well-maintained homes. In 1925 Hiawatha was cited by *The Mining Congress Journal* as one of the most modern and well-laid-out coal camps of its size in the United States. A company-owned dairy farm once supplied milk, butter, and other products to Hiawatha and other company camps in Carbon County. Hiawatha is still a company town.

Keetley (lead, zinc, and silver mining). Keetley was built shortly after World War I by the Park-Utah Mining Company, which later became the New Park Mining Company. It was another model community with well-constructed houses, well-planned streets, and a good water supply. An excellent boardinghouse and recreational hall were maintained by the company. In 1947 the New Park Mining Company began a new townsite where homes would be sold to employees, thus eliminating the company-town atmosphere. The new project was never completed, however.

Kenilworth (coal mining). Kenilworth was founded as a coal-mining town in 1908 by the Independent Coal and Coke Company. It was a typical mining town in which the company owned all houses, a store, boardinghouse, recreation hall, etc., and participated in various community recreational activities. In 1960 the Kenilworth mine closed. All the houses were sold to individual occupants, and the company store was sold to a private operator. Kenilworth was considered an unusually attractive mining community and reached a peak population of about 800.

172

Mohrland (coal mining). This coal-mining community was first established in 1901 by the Castle Valley Coal Company. The following year the site became the property of the Utah Fuel Company, and all buildings except the school house belonged to this firm. In 1929 the company employed one thousand men at Mohrland. The camp was abandoned in 1938.

Newhouse (copper mining). From the early 1900's until the 1920's, Newhouse was the residence of employees at the Cactus Mine in Beaver County. It was a rather modern mining camp, for its time. The mine was developed by Samuel Newhouse, one of Utah's most prominent mining industrialists, and the town was named for him.

Rains (coal mining). The mine at Rains was opened in 1916 by L. F. Rains. The company was known as the Carbon Fuel Company. The Hi-Heat Coal Company later took over. The company owned all homes and operated a company store. The living area consisted of a few houses on either side of a single dirt road. It was not a model mining community, and former residents describe it as typical of the less desirable coal towns. The town has been abandoned since the 1940's.

Spring Canyon (coal mining). First named Storrs, Spring Canyon was established by the Spring Canyon Coal Company about 1912. Jesse Knight, prominent Utah businessman, was owner of the company. The town was well built with substantial sandstone houses, a good water system, sewerage, and other modern conveniences not yet installed in many coal camps. Knight owned and controlled all property and would sell none of it except for purposes approved by him. In 1922 James B. Smith and associates bought the Spring Canyon Coal Company. The company still owns the property, but mining ceased in 1958. In 1962 only about ten men were still employed, leaving Spring Canyon virtually abandoned. At the height of its activity Spring Canyon reached a population of about 1,000.

Standardville (coal mining). The second mine to be opened in the Spring Canyon area was opened by the Standard Coal Company in 1913. The town of Standardville was well constructed and maintained good sanitary conditions. It was a planned community, and in 1925 it was recognized by *The Mining Congress Journal* as far above average. Population at one time reached 1,000, but the town was abandoned several years ago when the company ceased operations.

Sunnyside and *Sunnydale* (coal mining). Sunnyside was founded about 1904 by the Utah Fuel Company. It was fully paternalistic, with the company owning the store, all homes, amusement hall, and all other recreational facilities. Even though it is still a company town, it was incorporated under Utah municipal laws in 1913 and is operated with a mayor and council as a municipal corporation. By World War II, Sunnyside had become practically a ghost town. In that year Utah Fuel Company leased its No. 2 mine to the Kaiser Company, Inc., which is the present Kaiser Steel Corporation. Feeling that the old homes were not adequate for modern needs, the Utah Fuel Company erected a new, modern housing area one mile from the old townsite, calling it Sunnydale. Sunnydale became an attractive, well-built residential area with all modern facilities. Since shopping and civic facilities were still located at Sunnyside, the company instituted a bus service which made scheduled trips to the shopping center and theater. Round-trip fee was ten cents. A branch of the company store was later established at Sunnydale. So attractive were the new housing facilities that residents of Sunnyside now put their names on the waiting list to move into the new section. In 1950 Kaiser purchased all the Utah Fuel Company property at Sunnyside. The area still operates as a company-owned community and all comes under the name of Sunnyside. Coal from the mine is coked and shipped for use to Kaiser's steel plant at Fontana, California.

Wattis (coal mining). Wattis grew around a coal mine begun in

1916 by the Wattis brothers and a man named Browning. In 1916 the camp and mine were sold to the Lion Coal Company. Housing accommodations were somewhat inadequate for many years. During World War II new apartment units, called "Wattis Villa," were erected, and the old boardinghouse was later condemned. Lion Coal Company still owns all homes at Wattis, renting them for as low as $29.00 a month. No business facilities exist at the present time.

Winter Quarters (coal mining). Winter Quarters, located in Carbon County, was the site of the first coal mine in Utah east of the Wasatch Mountains. A thriving camp was operating before the end of the nineteenth century, and in the early 1900's more miners' cottages were added. The settlement, owned by Pleasant Valley Coal Company, was abandoned after the mine closed in 1928.

Washington

Black Diamond (coal mining). Black Diamond was a company-owned community, but private parties were able to lease ground for one hundred dollars a year and build their own homes. Private businesses also operated. Black Diamond was established in the 1880's by the Black Diamond Mining Company when its operations near Nortonville, California, were being threatened by high-grade coal from Washington. A serious strike in the 1920's, together with a decline in demand for coal in later years, brought Black Diamond virtually to a standstill as far as mining was concerned. The town was incorporated, however, in 1959.

Bordeaux (logging camp and lumber mill). This camp was founded by the Bordeaux brothers in the 1890's. At its peak it employed over seven hundred men. In 1941 the mill was closed, and Bordeaux became a ghost town.

Carbonado (coal mining). Carbonado was an old-time company town which, in the 1950's, was given up as a ghost town.

175

Residents, however, bought their own homes from the company, found employment in nearby mines and logging operations, and have created an independent community.

Doty (lumber mill). Doty was a company town which was closed in the 1930's because of operating difficulties.

Dryad (lumber mill). Dryad was a lumber-mill town established in the latter nineteenth century by Leudinghaus Lumber Company. Most of the houses were owned by the company, although other businesses were also allowed to operate hotels, cafes, saloons, etc. Houses were built in rows and all of the same style. The town was once a lively community of about 1,000 people. In the 1920's it was purchased by March & Duncan. This company sold it to Schaeffer Brothers in 1937. The latter firm operated the mill for only a short time before junking the mill and houses in 1939. A few houses were sold to residents, but most were torn down.

DuPont (explosives plant). DuPont was established in 1906–1907 by the E. I. Du Pont de Nemours and Company to house employees at its Washington powder plant. Properties were sold to occupants in the early 1950's, and the town was incorporated in 1951.

Fortson (lumber mill). Fortson, seven miles west of Darrington, was once a company-owned mill town. It is now abandoned.

Holden (copper mining). Holden was a company-owned town operated since the 1930's by the Howe Sound Mining Company. Lack of ore caused the mine to cease operating in 1957. In 1960 the entire town was donated to the Seattle Lutheran Bible Institute.

Longview (lumber mill). This town was never a real company town. It is mentioned here only as an example of the trend of some companies to build entire towns specifically to sell to employees and business people with the idea of making them permanent, independent communities. Longview was such a town, created in the 1920's.

McCleary (lumber mill). McCleary was founded in 1898 as a

176

logging camp and mill town for the Henry McCleary Timber Company. In 1941 it was sold to Simpson Logging Company, which soon sold all the homes and got out of the company-town business. McCleary was incorporated in 1942.

Malone (lumber mill). Malone was established in the early 1900's by the Joe Vance Lumber Company. The company did very well and later sold out to the Bordeaux Lumber Company. The mill was closed during the depression, and houses were sold for whatever they would bring.

Montezuma (lumber mill). Montezuma was a full-fledged company town operated by the Manley-Moore Lumber Company from 1910 to 1935. Peak population was 500–600, and all employees of the mill were housed at the town. It was forty miles from Tacoma, the closest major center of population. The closing of the mill in 1935 brought an end to the town.

National (lumber mill). National was established as a sawmill town by the Pacific National Lumber Company in the first decade of this century. It was a fully-owned company town, although it was only one and one-half miles from Ashford, the nearest village. During World War II the property was sold to Harbor Plywood Company, and the mill was dismantled. The town was improved and continued, however, as logging continued. The Weyerhaeuser Company later purchased the town but discontinued it, maintaining only the logging operations. Most of the buildings were sold for removal.

Newcastle (coal mining). Newcastle was an early coal-mining company-owned town which boasted three hundred houses, a store, and a hotel. Its original name was Coal Creek, but after World War I it was changed. By 1947 it had become practically a ghost town, with homes having been sold to residents.

Onalaska (lumber mill). Onalaska was a company-owned town of the Carlisle Lumber Company. In the 1940's it had a population of around 1,200. By 1960 the population had slipped to 210.

Ostrander (logging and lumber mill). Ostrander originally was established in the 1880's as a logging operation by Mr. A. B. Root, of Pennsylvania, backed by a family named Collins. In later years E. S. Collins took charge and formed the Ostrander Railway and Timber Company, which became a million-dollar concern. There were about thirty-four homes in Ostrander, all but two owned by the company. There was also a company store and a Methodist church. It was a quiet little community, and Collins quickly removed anyone who drank to excess or became a trouble maker. In 1939 the lack of timber caused the company to cease operations. The mill was junked, and more than half the houses were given to long-time employees. Other houses were sold at small cost to new employees who were living in them.

Port Gamble (lumber mill). Port Gamble is probably the longest lived company town in the West. It was established in 1853 by Pope & Talbot. Its excellent location and picturesque New England architecture helped make it a particularly attractive community. The town still exists, and although the company does not need to operate it, the plan is to maintain at least the main street as a landmark.

Port Ludlow (lumber mill). Pope & Talbot purchased the Port Ludlow Mill Company, and with it the small company-owned settlement, in 1878. The company did not begin operations until 1884, after which it became another flourishing mill town of the Puget Mill Company, a subsidiary of Pope & Talbot. Port Ludlow continued operating until 1945 when it was decided that, because of the decline of timber, two mills should not be operated in such close proximity. The company still owns the site, but everything is closed at present.

Pysht (logging camp). Pysht was a small headquarters camp of the Merrill and Ring Logging Company from 1878 to 1944, with brief periods of discontinuance. It had only about fifteen houses and a small company store. It is only typical of scores of such camps which existed in the logging country and are not generally included here.

178

Roslyn (coal mining). Roslyn was founded in the 1880's by the Northern Pacific Coal Company, a subsidiary of the Northern Pacific Railroad. The first businesses were a company store and a company-owned saloon. The latter was operated because of the company's desire to regulate liquor traffic. In the early days houses built by the company rented very cheaply, but workers could also lease ground and build their own homes. Roslyn eventually expanded to become a large, bustling community of home owners and private businesses, and not a company town in the traditional sense. A few houses are still rented by the company, although the coal mine is no longer active. At the turn of the century Roslyn boasted a population of 4,000. The present population is only about 1,000.

Ryderwood (logging camp). Most logging camps were temporary bachelor communities with few facilities for families. Ryderwood was unusual, however, in that it was established by the Long-Bell Lumber Company in 1922 as a "family camp." It was felt that this would bring the company a more stable worker instead of the "boomers" or drifters common to logging operations. Ryderwood had 375 houses, a cook house, and a twenty-four-room school building which included all grades from kindergarten through high school. In 1952 logging was finished in the area, and the town was sold to Senior Estates, Inc., who turned it into a community for retired people.

Sappho (logging camp). Sappho was the logging headquarters of Bloedell-Donovan Lumber Company, which established their camp in 1924. A small settlement already existed, however, prior to this time. Sappho was a permanent-type logging community consisting of about twenty family houses and bunk houses for 250 to 300 men. The typical company store provided credit and would deduct from wages. In 1946 Rayonier, Inc., bought the holdings of Bloedel-Donovan, and this firm still operates the camp.

Seabeck (lumber mill). Seabeck was founded in 1856 by the Washington Mill Company. Edward Clayson, who owned property just outside the mill company property, was a particular thorn in the flesh of the managers of Seabeck, for he was constantly criticizing their alleged "slave" operation of the town. The burning of the mill in 1886 brought an end to the operation. The old houses, church, and hotel building have been restored, and the area now serves as a recreational center for church groups during the summer.

Snoqualmie Falls (lumber mill). Snoqualmie Falls was constructed in 1917–18 by the Snoqualmie Falls Lumber Company, later a branch of the Weyerhaeuser Company. At one time the town consisted of 225 company-owned dwellings. The company provided a community hall, hospital, water, garbage collection, and electric power. It also ran a company store until 1955. At its peak the settlement had a population of about 900, approximately 65 per cent of the company's employees. In 1957 the company houses were sold to employees, who moved them into the town of Snoqualmie. There were only twenty-two company-owned dwellings remaining in Snoqualmie Falls in 1962.

Three Lakes (lumber mill). The Three Lakes Lumber Company was founded in 1903. The company-owned town was abandoned in the 1920's when the surrounding timber had been cut out.

Tono (coal mining). In 1907 the Union Pacific Coal Company jumped to Washington and incorporated the Washington Union Coal Company, owners of the site of Tono, as a subsidiary. In 1932 the settlement was taken over by the Bucoda Coal Mining Company.

Vail (logging headquarters). Vail was founded in 1928 by the Weyerhaeuser Company as a center of its logging operations. Several additional camps existed in the woods, but Vail was the central, permanent camp. The company built fifty-two houses and several bunkhouses for single men. It also had a company store, which closed in 1952. Vail is still owned by the company, although the cook houses, bunkhouses, and company store are gone because of the changing economic pattern of the logging business.

Wyoming

Carbon (coal mining). Established in 1868, Carbon was the first coal-mining town to be created by the Union Pacific Coal Company. It was not an ordinary company town, for miners owned their own homes. It is mentioned as an example of the early Wyoming mining communities which led eventually to the establishment of company towns. A company store existed in town, and the community also had a company doctor. It was disbanded in 1902.

Cumberland (coal mining). This mining town, established by Union Pacific Coal Company shortly after 1900, closed in 1930.

Frontier (coal mining). This coal-mining camp was established in 1897 to provide housing for the Kemmerer Coal Company's mine at Frontier. The Uintah Improvement Company, which owned the land, the Kemmerer Coal Company, which produced the coal, the Frontier Supply Company, which was the company store, and the Lincoln Service Corporation, which provided utilities, were all part of the same holding corporation. At Frontier the company owned most of the houses, although individuals could lease land and build their own homes if they wished. Frontier is still company owned, although no store and only a few houses still exist. No coal mining is going on at the present time. Frontier is adjacent to Kemmerer, which was established about one year after Frontier. Frontier was Kemmerer Coal Company's first mine.

Diamondville (coal mining). Diamondville was the site of a mine established by the Diamond Coal & Coke Company about 1892. It operated until about 1940.

Elco (coal mining). The Elco mine of the Kemmerer Coal Company was the scene of a small settlement of about twenty houses and a company store in the early part of this century.

Dana (coal mining). This small settlement adjacent to a mine of the Union Pacific Coal Company lasted for only three or four years early in this century.

Hanna (coal mining). Hanna was an outstanding community

of the Union Pacific Coal Company. Established in 1889, it was fully paternalistic, with the company owning all homes, providing all recreational facilities, assisting in the erection of churches, and operating a company store. About 1950 the last mine at Hanna closed. Homes were then sold to employees who wanted to stay in the town, and many of these workers remain. The property still belongs to the company.

Midwest (oil wells and refinery). Midwest was a large company town of the Midwest Refining Company. It flourished early in this century and consisted of a main settlement and several auxiliary camps.

Reliance (coal mining). Reliance was founded in 1910 by the Union Pacific Coal Company. It consisted of about 145 homes, a company store, three boardinghouses, and other community facilities. In 1954 the Reliance mines were closed because the railroad was converting to diesel fuel. The company store was closed, and most of the houses were sold to residents.

Sinclair (oil refining). Originally called Parco, this town was begun in 1922 by the Producers and Refiners Corporation, which built a large oil refinery here. In 1934 the refinery and town were purchased by the Sinclair Oil Corporation. The town is fully owned by Sinclair, although business facilities are leased to private operators. The homes are substantial, attractive structures, and the whole town gives the appearance of a well-planned, pleasant community.

Sublet #5 (coal mining). Kemmerer Coal Company's mine called Sublet #5 was supported by a company-owned settlement of about 500 people served by a company store.

Sublet #6 (coal mining). Kemmerer Coal Company's mine called Sublet #6 was supported by a small company-owned settlement of about 200 people. It had about thirty-five houses and a company store.

Susie (coal mining). The small Susie mine of the Kemmerer

182

Coal Company was the scene of a tiny company-owned settlement of about fifteen houses and a small store.

Sunrise (iron mining). Sunrise was the scene of Colorado Fuel and Iron Corporation's large Wyoming iron mines. The first ore was shipped in 1899. In 1902 the company employed 153 men in the mines. Several new brick homes were in the process of being erected. The town had a school and a branch of the Colorado Supply Company store.

Superior (coal mining). Mines at Superior were opened by the Union Pacific Coal Company about 1905. The town was first called Reliance, but the name was changed to Superior in 1906. The closing of the mine in 1962 brought to an end the last large coal-mining operation in the Rock Springs-Superior area.

Winton (coal mining). Winton, near Rock Springs, was established in 1917 by the Megeath Coal Company. It was purchased in 1921 by the Union Pacific Coal Company, although the town and mines had been partly on Union Pacific property anyway. Winton was an unusual mining community in a number of respects. First, it was a model town, well planned and designed from the beginning. Next, the community council, a body made up of representatives of various employee groups, acted almost as a governing agency, even though the town was not incorporated and the company was still in charge.

W HILE it is usually the function of a bibliography to give full publication or other reference data on sources specifically cited in the text, another purpose is also considered of value here. In addition to the sources cited in the footnotes, the writer relied heavily upon important background information and general impressions drawn from many other sources. In the text, for example, certain company-owned towns were singled out to illustrate certain generalizations. These generalizations, however, were arrived at on the basis of information obtained from many more towns, but it would have been impractical to cite all additional references or sources, or to multiply examples in the text. It was felt, however, that some of these additional sources should be made known to the interested reader and that the appropriate method of doing this was in connection with the standard bibliography. The normal pattern, therefore, has been modified in order to make this bibliography more meaningful to anyone who may wish to pursue the topic further. The bibliography has been divided into eight categories. Listed first in each category are the references specifically cited in the text. Then follows a brief essay describing some of the other sources which were especially useful in providing background or forming conclusions.

U.S. Government Publications

" 'Industrial Necessity' for Political Control: An Incident of the Colorado Miner's Strike," *Monthly Labor Review*, Vol. III, No. 2 (August, 1916).

Magnusson, Leifur. "Company Housing in the Bituminous Coal Fields," *Monthly Labor Review*, Vol. X, No. 4 (April, 1920).

―――. "A Modern Copper Mining Town," *Monthly Labor Review*, Vol. VII, No. 3 (September, 1918).

―――. "Sanitary Aspects of Company Housing," *Monthly Labor Review*, Vol. VIII, No. 1 (January, 1919).

"Report of the Colorado Coal Commission," *Monthly Labor Review*, Vol. II, No. 4 (April, 1916).

U.S. Coal Commission (John Hays Hammond, chairman). *Report of the United States Coal Commission, Dec. 10, 1923*. Washington, Government Printing Office, 1925.

U.S. Coal Mines Administration. *A Medical Survey of the Bituminous Coal Industry. Report of the Coal Mines Administration*. Washington, Government Printing Office, 1947.

"Welfare Work in Company Towns," *Monthly Labor Review*, Vol. XXV, No. 2 (August, 1927).

The most extensive federal survey of company houses in the United States was compiled in 1920 by Leifur Magnusson and published as Bulletin No. 263 of the Bureau of Labor Statistics, under the title *Housing by Employers in the United States*. Although this report contains only two short sections on mining towns in the West, and completely neglects lumber company towns, it is most valuable in its excellent presentation of the general development of company housing projects in a variety of industries throughout the United States. Its conclusions concerning company housing in the West generally agree with those in the present study. It includes a valuable list of references, mostly pertaining to Eastern and Southern projects, and an interesting list of representative companies maintaining housing for employees.

In addition to the items cited above, the following articles from the *Monthly Labor Review* are helpful: "Adjustment of Labor Difficulties in the Arizona Copper Region," Vol. V, No. 6 (December, 1917); "Company Stores and the Scrip System," Vol. XLI,

No. 1 (July, 1935); "Investigation of Wage Payments in Scrip," Vol. XXXVIII, No. 5 (May, 1934); "Legislation Relating to Payment of Wages in Scrip, Protection of Employees as Traders, and Company Stores," Vol. XLIII, No. 1 (July, 1936); and "Reduction of Cost of Living by Company Stores in Arizona," Vol. XVI, No. 4 (1923).

Company Publications

The Brine Line. Periodical published by American Potash and Chemical Corp.

Camp and Plant. Periodical published by Colorado Fuel and Iron Corp., 1901–1905.

Colorado Fuel and Iron Industrial Bulletin.

Holbrook, Stewart. *Green Commonwealth.* Shelton, Wash., Simpson Logging Co., 1950.

The Midwest Review. Periodical published by the Midwest Refining Co.

Phelps Dodge Corporation. *Annual Report.* 1957, 1961.

The Struggle in Colorado For Industrial Freedom. Bulletin issued periodically by coal operators in Colorado during the 1914 labor difficulties.

Train, Arthur, Jr. *Ajo.* Published privately by Phelps Dodge Corp., 1941.

The Trona Argonaut. Former periodical published by American Potash and Chemical Corp.

In addition to these items specifically cited in the text, many companies have published periodicals to be circulated among their employees, and these reflect much about the towns involved. Company propaganda brochures are also *sometimes* helpful in providing background and basic chronology. Among some of the most useful company publications are the following: *The Dawson News* (published by Phelps Dodge Corp., 1921–29); *The Story of Goodyear Farms* (information brochure published by Goodyear Tire and Rubber Co.); *Kennecott Chinorama* (periodical published by Kennecott Copper Corp.); *The Utah Copper Story* (brochure published by Kennecott Copper Corp., Utah Copper Division); *The Log of Long-Bell* (75th anniversary publication of Long-Bell Lumber Co., 1950); *Scotia: Home of The Pacific Lumber Company* (published by Pacific Lumber Co., 1961); *Sinclair Dealer News*; Arthur Train, Jr., *Bisbee*, and Arthur Train, Jr., *Morenci* (both published by Phelps Dodge Corp., 1941); *The Trona Potash* (first weekly publication of American Potash and Chemical Corp.); and *You and Your Company* (pamphlet published by Anaconda Co., Weed Heights, Nev.).

Correspondence

Perhaps the most fruitful source of information for this study was the personal correspondence and personal interviews conducted with scores of individuals who had been connected with company towns. This represented a wide cross section of employees and of management personnel, as well as people who had been connected with company towns in other ways. Listed below are some of the people who wrote personal letters to the author or who answered a general questionnaire sent them by the author. This includes those cited in the text as well as others whose letters were of special interest:

Hank Abraham (forester, Mt. Whitney Lumber Co., Johnsondale, Calif., February, 1962); B. Z. Agrons (general manager, Rockport Redwood Co., Rockport, Calif., May 5, 1962); Harold T. Allen (Logan, Utah, April 11, 1963); R. E. Andrews (Comptroller's Department, Kennecott Copper Corp., Chino Mines Division, Hurley, N.M., June 25, 1962); Jerome P. Arends (Publicity Department, American Forest Products Corp., San Francisco, Calif., May 16, 1962); Philip J. Atkinson (Sappho, Wash., June, 1962); M. E. Barron (resident manager, Fruit Growers Supply Co., Hilt, Calif., February, 1962); D. E. Bornstedt (Longview, Wash., November 19, 1962; December 21, 1962); James P. Bradley (president, Bradley Mining Co., San Francisco, Calif., July 26,

1962); Mrs. Harold Brower (Hood River, Ore., June 11, 1962); Samuel H. Brown (Public Affairs Department, Weyerhaeuser Co., Tacoma, Wash., May 23, 1962); Ralph Busby (postmaster, Malone, Wash., May, 1962); Lester E. Calder (regional land supervisor, Weyerhaeuser Co., Springfield, Ore., July 5, 1962); L. M. Carter (Westfir, Ore., May, 1962); Vernon D. Chamberlin (general manager, Feather River Pine Mills Co., Feather Falls, Calif., June 12, 1962); W. W. Clark (Portland, Ore., May 22, 1962); Carl L. Davis (Portland, Ore., May 31, 1962); Richard H. Eddy (engineer, Pickering Lumber Co., Standard, Calif., February 13, 1962); Willard Evenson (president, Wauna Lumber Co., Wauna, Ore., May 31, 1962); Dale Fischer (Eugene, Ore., May 24, 1962); Susie Fountain (Arcata, Calif., February 19, 1962); William R. Gibbs (Reliance, Wyo., May 20, 1962); Jack M. Gruber (publications manager, Potlatch Forests, Inc., Lewiston, Idaho, May 14, 1962); Ramsay S. Harris (Phoenix, Ariz., July, 1962); E. N. Hausner (manager, Sinclair Refining Co., Sinclair, Wyo., January 29, 1962); Fred K. Hefferly (secretary-treasurer, United Mine Workers of America, Denver, Colo., April 18, 1962); Oscar Huber (general manager, Albuquerque & Cerrillos Coal Co., Albuquerque, N.M., June 11, 1962; June 17, 1962); W. H. Hutchinson (Chico, Calif., May 28, 1962); Dave James (director of public affairs, Simpson Timber Co., Seattle, Wash., March 12, 1962; May 25, 1962); Sam Knight (Tucson, Ariz., April, 1962); H. Laturner (Price, Utah, April, 1963); William O. Lewis (Bremerton, Wash., July 11, 1962); H. A. Libby (president, Arcata Redwood Co., Arcata, Calif., March 6, 1962); E. F. Marchetti (postmaster, Helper, Utah, February, 1963); John W. Marshall (Westend, Calif., February 1962); Marie P. Mickelson (Chester, Calif., May, 1962); A. E. Millar (general manager, Anaconda Co., Weed Heights, Nev., May 14, 1962); Russell C. Miller (community manager, Climax Molybdenum Co., Climax, Colo., April 10, 1962); Ed C. Morrison (Hornitos, Calif., May 27, 1962); K. M. Murdock (secretary-manager, Pacific Northwest Loggers Association, Seattle, Wash., February 7, 1962); Frank Musso (Roslyn, Wash., May 29, 1962); Tom Mutchler (public relations manager, International Paper Co., Long-Bell Division, Longview, Wash., May 21, 1962); George Neils (Libby, Mont., June 9, 1962); A. T. Newell (consultant, Staufer Chemical Co., Henderson, Nev., April 13, 1962); Mrs. Ted Newell (Sunnyside, Utah, February, 1963); Harry B. Onn (Chehalis, Wash., May, 1962); Algird C. Pocius (director of publicity, Colorado Fuel and Iron Corp., Pueblo, Colorado, August 2, 1962; September 11, 1962); J. D. Pressett (Dragerton, Utah, February, 1963); Arthur W. Priaulx (public relations director, West Coast Lumbermen's Assoc., Portland, Ore., February 6, 1962); Fred Reicker (administrative assistant, Public Relations, Kaiser Steel Corp., Fontana, Calif., August 13, 1962); Louis J. Rexroth (Gig Harbor, Wash., May, 1962); Obert E. Rye (Colstrip, Mont., August, 1962); R. P. Saffold, Jr. (director, Public Relations, Kennecott Copper Corp., Chino Mines Division, Hurley, N.M., January 29, 1962; April 3, 1962); Selwyn J. Sharp (secretary, California Redwood Assoc., San Francisco, Calif., February 14, 1962); J. E. Shipsey (manager, Diamond National Corp., Red Bluff, Calif., May 17, 1962); Mrs. Jennie Snider (Vail, Wash., June, 1962); D. K. Stark (industrial relations representative, Kennecott Copper Corp., Nevada Mines Division, McGill, Nev., February 23, 1962; June 6, 1962); E. E. Stewart (special assistant to production manager, E. I. Du Pont de Nemours & Co., Wilmington, Del., June 6, 1962; June 18, 1962); Moses C. Taylor (Kamas, Utah, July 18, 1962); Ernest C. Teagle (McCleary, Wash., June, 1962); Maurice Thon (chief accountant, Bagdad Copper Corp., Bagdad, Ariz., August 17, 1962); Hamp Wilson (general manager, Gallup Gamerco Coal Co., Gamerco, N.M., February, 1962); Jack E. Woods (attorney, Richfield Oil Corp., Los Angeles, Calif., February 6, 1962); Ray Woods (Kearny, Ariz., April, 1962).

Personal Interviews

These interviews were all conducted by the writer, and all persons interviewed had some direct connection with company towns. Interviews listed below include those cited in the text as well as the most helpful additional interviews obtained:

B. Z. Agrons (general manager, Rockport Redwood Co., Rockport, Calif., April 13, 1962); Alden Ball (public relations representative, Pacific Lumber Co., Scotia, Calif., April 18, 1962); H. C. Beall (manager, Phelps Dodge Mercantile Co., Bisbee, Ariz., March 13, 1962); Charles J. Bella (Santa Cruz, Calif., May 4, 1962); J. A. Briggs (manager, New Cornelia Branch, Phelps Dodge Corp., Ajo, Ariz., March 23, 1962); James Bryson (general manager, Valsetz Division, Boise Cascade Corp., Portland, Ore., April 25, 1962); Mr. and Mrs. O. C. Buehler (Hanna, Wyo., July 6, 1961); Dave Davis (personnel manager, Simpson Timber Co., Korbel, Calif., April 16, 1962); Emanuel Fritz (professor emeritus, School of Forestry, University of California, Berkeley, Calif., April 11, 1962); Gerald H. Galbreath, Jr. (John W. Galbreath & Co., Columbus, Ohio, interviewed at Kearny, Ariz., March 8, 1962); M. C. Gerlicher (assistant manager, McCloud River Lumber Co., McCloud, Calif., April 20, 1962); Mr. and Mrs. William Goldman (Los Angeles, Calif., June 24, 1961); Nathan E. Guire (Hayden, Ariz., March 8, 1962); J. Rodney Hastings (first mayor of Hayden, Ariz. Interviewed at Tucson, Ariz., March 21, 1962); R. A. Hood (Albion, Calif., April 13, 1962); Donald R. Jameson (plant superintendent, American Smelting and Refining Co., Silver Bell, Ariz., March 22, 1962); Mr. and Mrs. Henry Jones (Laramie, Wyo., July 8, 1961); George Knab (Arcata Redwood Co., Arcata, Calif., April 18, 1962); W. Newell Kring (vice-president, Goodyear Farms, Litchfield Park, Ariz., March 16, 1962); A. O. Lefors (secretary, California Redwood Assoc., San Francisco, Calif., April 10, 1962); J. A. Lentz (manager, Morenci Branch, Phelps Dodge Corp., Morenci, Ariz.,

190

March 14, 1962); James W. Lilley (superintendent, Caspar Lumber Co., Caspar, Calif., April 13, 1962); James A. McArthur, Jr. (Samoa, Calif., April 19, 1962); John W. McClean (employment agent, Phelps Dodge Corp., New Cornelia Branch, Ajo, Ariz., March 23, 1962); Mr. and Mrs. Floyd Mack (Phoenix, Ariz., March 17, 1962); John W. Marshall (Calimesa, Calif., February 19, 1962); Frederick Marsic (secretary, American Potash and Chemical Corp., Los Angeles, Calif., May 19, 1960); Charles D. Michaelson (general manager, Western Mining Division, Kennecott Copper Corp., Salt Lake City, Utah, August 8, 1961); Mrs. Elsie Miller (Arcata, Calif., April 19, 1962); H. E. Moore (office manager, Phelps Dodge Corp., Douglas, Ariz., March 12, 1962); Roy F. Morse (former vice-president, Long-Bell Lumber Co., Longview, Wash., April 27, 1962); V. O. Murray (president and general manager, Union Pacific Coal Co., Rock Springs, Wyo., July 6, 1961); George W. Nelson (former chief inspector, California Redwood Assoc., Eureka, Calif., April 14–17, 1962); R. B. Nichols (manager, Arcata & Mad River Railroad, Blue Lake, Calif., April 16, 1962); Patricia Paylore (Tucson, Ariz., March 20, 1962); Harold Potter (project manager for John W. Galbreath & Co., Kearny, Ariz., March 7, 1962); R. R. Roberts (Portland, Ore., May 29, 1962); Mrs. Mary Scanlon (chief clerk, Phelps Dodge Mercantile Co., Morenci, Ariz., March 14, 1962); Mrs. Jane Sewell (Hayden, Ariz., March 8, 1962); Selwyn J. Sharp (secretary, retired, California Redwood Assoc., San Francisco, Calif., April 10, 1962); Ted Shelton (rental agent, Phelps Dodge Corp., Ajo, Ariz., March 23, 1962); H. Lee Smith (general manager, Phelps Dodge Mercantile Co., Douglas, Ariz., March 13, 1962); George H. Sturtevant (public relations officer, American Potash and Chemical Corp., Los Angeles, Calif., May 19, 1960); Mrs. Irene F. Tallis (Hilt, Calif., May 2, 1962); Emil Talvola (Eureka, Calif., April 16, 1962); P. M. Vallero (chief clerk, Phelps Dodge Corp., Morenci Branch, Morenci, Ariz., March 14, 1962); Cyrus T. Walker (vice-president, Pope & Tal-

191

bot, Inc., Portland, Ore., April 26, 1962); John Whiston (Kemmerer, Wyo., July 5, 1961); J. M. White (former president, Long-Bell Lumber Co., Weed, Calif., April 10, 1962); Mr. and Mrs. Ivan K. Willard (Ajo, Ariz., March 22, 1962); W. J. Wrigley (former president, Elk River Mill & Lumber Co., Falk, Calif., April 16, 1962); John Zivnuska (professor of forestry, University of California, Berkeley, Calif., April 11, 1962).

Additional Unpublished Material

Arizona Copper Co., "Cost Statement" for the year ended September 30, 1920. In Arizona Copper Co. papers at the University of Arizona, Tucson, Arizona.

Brogdon, J. Carl. "The History of Jerome, Arizona." Unpublished Master's thesis, Department of History, University of Arizona, 1952.

Del Castillo, José. Manuscript collection on Arizona. Filed at the library of the Pioneer Historical Society of Arizona, Tucson, Ariz.

Cross, Clark Irwin. "Factors Influencing the Abandonment of Lumber Mill Towns in the Puget Sound Region." Unpublished Master's thesis, School of Forestry, University of Washington, 1946.

Jeffrey, Robert S. "The History of Douglas, Arizona." Unpublished Master's thesis, Department of History, University of Arizona, 1951.

Leonard, John W. "The Economics of a One-Industry Town." Unpublished Master's thesis, College of Business and Public Administration, University of Arizona, 1954.

Poston, Charles D. MS for a speech apparently delivered in 1896. Typewritten copy on file at Pioneer Historical Society of Arizona, Tucson, Ariz.

Richins, Lucile. "A Social History of Sunnyside." Utah Historical Records Survey, March, 1940. Typewritten MS filed at Utah State Historical Society, Salt Lake City, Utah.

Riddell, E. E. "History of Seabeck." Mimeographed MS, revised 1952.

Saffold, R. P., Jr. Speech delivered before Highlands University Workshop at Las Vegas, N.M., August 8, 1961.

Smith, Susan M. "Litchfield Park and Vicinity." Unpublished Master's thesis, Department of History, University of Arizona, 1948.

Watt, Roberta. "History of Morenci, Arizona." Unpublished Master's thesis, Department of History, University of Arizona, 1956.

Weed Lumber Company. "Monthly Report," December, 1911; "Annual Report," 1911. With Weed Lumber Co. papers, Bancroft Library, University of California, Berkeley, Calif.

It is difficult to obtain access to the official records of most companies, but the papers of a few old companies, whose operations are now abandoned, have found their way into the archives of some university libraries and state historical societies. Miscellaneous papers from the old Twin Buttes Mining & Smelting Co., for example, are housed at the University of Arizona Library. The Washington Mill Co. papers are located at the University of Washington. Papers of the Grass Creek Coal Co. are housed at the L.D.S. Church Historian's Office in Salt Lake City, Utah. Unfortunately, however, such collections of papers usually reveal little of the operations of company towns. More helpful are the typewritten histories of certain towns which have sometimes been placed in various libraries. These are usually written by former residents, and present a one-side picture. Another interesting source of information is the Union Lumber Company Museum at Fort Bragg, California, which contains pictures of many former mill towns in the immediate area and brief information on each of them.

Books

Allen, Hugh. *The House of Goodyear: A Story of Rubber and of Modern Business.* Cleveland, Corday & Gross Co., 1943.

Beshoar, Barron R. *Out of the Depths: The Story of John R. Lawson a Labor Leader*. Denver, Colorado Labor and Historical Committee of the Denver Trades and Labor Assembly, 1943.

Clayson, Edward, Sr. *Historical Narrative of Puget Sound, Hoods Canal, 1865–1885: The Experience of an Only Free Man in a Penal Colony*. Seattle, R. L. Davis Printing Co., 1911.

Cleland, Robert Glass. *A History of Phelps Dodge, 1834–1950*. New York, Alfred A. Knopf, 1952.

Coman, Edwin T., Jr., and Helen Gibbs. *Time, Tide and Timber: A Century of Pope and Talbot*. Stanford, Stanford University Press, 1950.

Cooley, H. B. *Story of a Complete Modern Coal Mine*. Reprint in booklet form of a series of articles in *Coal Age*, August-September, 1923.

Gressinger, A. W. *Charles D. Poston, Sunland Seer*. Globe, Dale Stuart King, 1961.

History of the Union Pacific Coal Mines, 1896 to 1940. Omaha, Colonia Press, 1940.

Hopkins, Ernest J. *Financing the Frontier: A Fifty Year History of the Valley National Bank*. Phoenix, Arizona Printers, Inc., 1950.

Johnson, Ole S. *The Industrial Store*. Atlanta, Research Division, School of Business Administration, Atlanta Division, University of Georgia, 1952.

Knight, Jesse William. *The Jesse Knight Family*. Salt Lake City, Deseret News Press, 1941.

McArthur, Lewis A. *Oregon Geographic Names*. Portland, Binfords & Mort, 1952.

McClelland, John M., Jr. *Longview . . . The Remarkable Beginnings of a Modern Western City*. Portland, Binfords & Mort, 1949.

Marcosson, Isaac F. *Anaconda*. New York, Dodd, Mead & Co., 1957.

Morgan, George T., Jr. *William B. Greeley, A Practical Forester.* St. Paul, Forest History Society, Inc., 1961.

Reynolds, Thursey Jensen (comp.). *Centennial Echos from Carbon County.* Carbon County, Utah, Daughters of the Utah Pioneers, 1948.

Risser, Hubert E. *The Economics of the Coal Industry.* Lawrence, Kan., Bureau of Business Research, School of Business, University of Kansas, 1958.

Robie, Edward H. (ed.). *Economics of the Mineral Industries: A Series of Articles by Specialists.* New York, American Institute of Mining, Metallurgical and Petroleum Engineers, Inc., 1959.

Shurick, A. T. *The Coal Industry.* Boston, Little, Brown and Co., 1924.

Tuck, Frank J. (comp.). *History of Mining in Arizona.* Phoenix, Arizona Department of Mineral Resources, 1955.

West, George P. *U.S. Commission on Industrial Relations Report on the Colorado Strike.* Chicago, Barnard and Miller, 1915.

WPA Writers' Program. *New Mexico: A Guide to the Colorful State.* New York, Hastings House, 1953.

———. *Wyoming: A Guide to Its History, Highways, and People.* New York, Oxford University Press, 1948.

County histories are sometimes useful in identifying company-owned towns and getting basic chronology, but they are not usually very scholarly or well documented. More useful are the WPA guides which were prepared for most of the Western states. They were usually prepared by competent scholars, and they give at least brief descriptions of most communities existing in the state at the time of the survey.

Articles and Periodicals

"Anaconda Copper Has Model Town at Conda, Idaho," *Engineering and Mining Journal,* Vol. CXXX, No. 5 (September 8, 1930).

The Arizona Republican

Blank, Joseph P. "He Turned Company Towns into Home Towns," *American Business*, Vol. XXVIII, No. 9 (September, 1958).

Casaday, L. W. "The Economics of a One-Industry Town. Review of a Bureau Study of Ajo," *Arizona Business and Economic Review*, Vol. III, No. 12 (December, 1954).

"Company Town, 1956," *Time* (April 16, 1956).

Cosulich, Bernice. "When Old Tubac was Young and Prosperous," *Arizona Daily Star*, February 21, 1932.

Culver, Virginia. "Tokens of Trona a Bygone Epoch," *Coin World* (February 23, 1962).

The Denver Post

Graham, Frank E. "Complete Motor Fire Department Protects California Mill," *The Timberman*, Vol. XXII, No. 3 (January, 1921).

The Herald Democrat (Leadville, Colorado).

Johnson, Judith M. "Some Materials for Pacific Northwest History. Washington Mill Company Papers," *Pacific Northwest Quarterly*, Vol. V, No. 3 (July, 1960).

The McCleary Stimulator. Special edition, December 4, 1958.

McDonald, John. "Georgia Pacific: It Grows Big on Trees," *Fortune*, Vol. LXV, No. 5 (May, 1962).

Murray, A. L. "Welfare and Safety in Connection with Mining in Utah," *The Mining Congress Journal*, Vol. XI, No. 10 (October, 1925).

The Salt Lake Tribune

"A Salute to Climax Molybdenum," special supplement to *Empire*, the magazine of *The Denver Post*, Sunday, May 23, 1954.

The Searles Review

The Seattle Times

Spencer, William. "Copperton—A Model Home Town for Utah Copper Employees," *Engineering and Mining Journal*, Vol. CXXV, No. 9 (March 3, 1928).

"Spotless Town," *Arizona*, Vol. VI, No. 6 (April, 1916).

"Switch Away from Paternalism Pays Off for Company, Workers, Town," *Chemical Week*, Vol. LXXXI, No. 20 (November 16, 1957).

Taylor, Frank J. "Paradise with a Waiting List," *Saturday Evening Post* (February 24, 1951).

"Too Much Town; Kennecott Copper Corp. Balks at Incorporation of Hayden, Arizona," *Business Week* (April 6, 1957).

United Mine Workers Journal, Vol. LX (April 1, 1949).

Willis, Charles F. "Housing at Tyrone, New Mexico," *Chemical and Metallurgical Engineering*, Vol. XIX, No. 8 (October 15, 1918).

Miscellaneous Items

State of Utah. *Report of the Coal Mine Inspector* (Title varies. Biennial reports since 1886).

"Working Agreement between the McCloud River Lumber Company and Town Sub Local Union No. 6–64 I.W.A.-C.I.O. McCloud, California" (1953).

An additional worth-while source of information is the clipping file usually kept by state historical societies. If one knows the name of a town or company, these files sometimes produce newspaper articles and other information of value. Files of the Oregon Historical Society, Pioneer Historical Society of Arizona, and Utah Historical Society were all used to good advantage in this study.

The Company Town in the American West has been cast on the Linotype in eleven-point Times Roman with three points of spacing between the lines. Handset Perpetua was selected for display to complement the Times Roman's contemporary character. The paper on which this book is printed is designed for an effective life of at least three hundred years and bears the watermark of the University of Oklahoma Press.